Shirley,

Life Is
All About
Range

Push New Boundaries!,

JP Coleman

Life Is
All About
Range

How to Replace Your Fears
with Knowledge and Skills

Jane Pastore Coleman

ISBN: 978-1-4834-0262-8 (sc)
ISBN: 978-1-4834-0264-2 (hc)
ISBN: 978-1-4834-0263-5 (e)

Library of Congress Control Number: 2013912840

Lulu Publishing Services rev. date: 07/26/2013

This book is dedicated to my angels, who look after me in all my adventures, and to my daring and adventurous husband "Bob", who always says you should replace your fears with knowledge and skills. I thank my husband for showing me a whole new world I never knew existed and for being patient with me through all the awkwardness of my learning curve.

Contents

Introduction

This is my personal story to share with others—the unlikely and extraordinary relationship that resulted from the chance meeting of two people having extremely different lifestyles. Being from very different backgrounds, we learned to respect and treasure our differences and committed to using those differences to expand the diversity of our life experiences. We call this "expanding our personal range."

This book started out as my personal diary in 2008, which allowed me to vent about my new life and experiences over the next three years. I had to deal with many of my fears to fit into my new world. I was confident in my own world, but when I arrived at Smokey Valley Farm, things started to unravel quickly.

I am a lifelong city girl who had to quickly assimilate the dramatically different world of Appalachian Kentucky and become a capable horsewoman. This book relates my experiences as I learned to manage my fears by acquiring knowledge and skills.

While the specifics of this story are unique to me, the lessons to be learned from my journey are relevant to all people who have yearned to cast off self-imposed boundaries and fears that prevent the expansion of their personal range, thereby opening doors to exciting new life experiences.

CHAPTER 1

Boy Meets Girl

This story begins in Scottsdale, Arizona, where I first met my husband, Bob, at a high-end sushi restaurant. At that time, we both had homes in Scottsdale.

We started talking. Bob asked me if I liked horses and proceeded to tell me he had a horse farm in Kentucky. He had actually brought some horses to Arizona to ride in the desert. Bob intrigued me. He was different from the men I had been meeting in Scottsdale. I had no idea that evening would lead to the life-altering events that soon followed.

When my dad retired from his job in New York, we made our pilgrimage to Florida, where most New Yorkers go to retire. There I was fortunate to live in an equestrian community called Horseshoe Acres, which gave me the opportunity to learn to ride well and to experience quarter horses. It had been many years since I'd talked about my passion for riding. I reflected back on my childhood and remembered the joy, solitude, and sense of well-being the horses had added to my life. The best part of riding a horse is that you have to be totally in the present, so your mind escapes any stress or worries about other things in life.

We continued to talk, and when Bob asked me if I wanted to go horseback riding for our first date, without hesitation, I quickly said,

"Yes!" I was excited to go riding, for I really enjoyed it, and I was excited to learn about the Tennessee Walking Horse breed.

At that time, I owned and ran a medical company. I hadn't ridden a horse in quite some time, since most of my energy and time were spent working. Ironically, my girlfriend who was with me that night quickly reminded me about my torn rotator cuff and asked how I would be able to ride. I turned to her and said, "As long as I can get on the horse, I can ride. Besides, it can't get any worse. It's already torn!"

Our first date was two days after we met at the sushi restaurant. I had never gone horseback riding on a first date, and I was also excited that we'd be riding in the desert, so this would be very different. We agreed to meet at a sandwich place prior to our ride to get sandwiches to pack for our picnic lunch.

When I first saw Bob's horses, I was in total awe; they were very different from the quarter horses I had owned. These Tennessee Walkers were lean and muscular in appearance. When I climbed in the saddle (with Bob's help due to my shoulder injury) and went for my first ride, I felt like I was floating on a cloud. I was amazed at how fast they could travel while performing their gaits.

We had a nice ride through the desert and even rode through a spot where there were lots of rattlesnakes, but we managed to get through it safely.

We had the most romantic first date. We stopped by a group of large boulders and had our picnic lunch in the desert in the midst of nature and all its glory on a beautiful sunny day. When Bob took me in his arms and kissed me for the first time, I felt like I was melting. At that moment, I knew I'd found my soul mate.

I had shoulder surgery the following week to repair my torn rotator cuff, and Bob was my private nurse. In the weeks that followed while I recovered, we talked about our shared experiences of starting medical companies and of our cultural differences and decided to become a couple.

The Proposal

One day Bob said, "We are going on a short trip for a couple of days, so I will help you pack your bag." The next thing I knew we were in Dana Point, California, on the beach. It was there that Bob hired an artist to build an unbelievable sand castle to proclaim his love. The castle had red rose petals scattered down the drawbridge and all around it. On the side of the castle were two hearts; one said, "Jane and Bob," and the other said, "Will you marry me?" At that moment, I was overcome with joy I had never known. I looked him in the eye and threw my one good arm over his shoulder, while my other arm was in its sling, and managed an awkward hug and said, "Yes."

This was the beginning of our storybook romance.

A few months later, Bob was going back to Kentucky for the summer and asked me to come along to see how I liked Kentucky and to meet his family. I accepted his invitation, closed up my home for the summer, packed up my two dogs, and headed to Kentucky. I could run my company from there by phone and fly back when I needed to. I had never been to Kentucky, so I was excited. I had no idea what lay ahead for me on this new venture in a place called Smokey Valley Farm.

CHAPTER 2

City Girl Goes Country

Personal Journal Entry, May 2008

It has been two weeks since I left Scottsdale, Arizona, to start my life with Bob, my fiancé, at Smokey Valley Farm in Kentucky. I feel so removed from the outside world in this safe haven of beauty I never knew about. This place called Kentucky has rolling hills and grass that is so green it looks blue; thus, they call it the Bluegrass State. I have lived in many big cities—New York, Los Angeles, Dallas, and Palm Beach—but here I definitely feel out of my element, with a whole new way of life to be explored as well as a new language to learn. I brought my two furry friends, Missy, a black-and-white shih tzu, and Tiffany, a teacup Yorkie.

When we got to the farmhouse, I met Bob's dogs, Nip and Tuck, miniature fox terriers who are sisters and as cute as can be. One day when I was walking around the farmhouse, Tuck charged out in front of me. As I looked down at my feet, I was horrified to see a big snake. Tuck, who is all of nine pounds, grabbed that snake and shook it like a rag doll. Well, that was enough to make me freak out. I called for Bob, but he was at the barn, so I ran into the house and called him on the phone. Bob came to my rescue, and, with a stick, he caught and released the snake to the creek behind the house. Tuck was fine. She was my little hero.

This was a lesson that taught me size does not matter and that you can tackle things bigger than you and not be afraid, as it's all in your attitude and approach. I later learned the black snake was harmless. Who knew?

When I first arrived at the farmhouse, I was wearing high heels and had my dogs in tow. I really was not prepared; when I got there, I learned that most of the roads were dirt and rock. So my struggling through the rugged terrain while holding both dogs to get to the farmhouse was quite the comedy act. I later told Bob that he would have to take me to a place I had heard about called Walmart to buy some flat shoes that would be more appropriate. The amazing part is that while I was accustomed to shopping at boutiques and stores like Nordstrom's, I was probably the only person in Kentucky who had never been inside a Walmart! As luck would have it, there was a Walmart superstore twenty-five minutes away. That was the closest and most popular store, not to mention my only choice.

I learned quickly not to wear white on a farm, for it's impossible to keep clean. Between the absence of Nordstrom's, trying to understand the language, and all the wildlife episodes, my perceptions quickly changed. I questioned this man I had met in Scottsdale who lived in this small town and who now spoke and dressed differently than when we met. I felt like Eva Gabor in Green Acres. All I could think about was her saying, "Good-bye, city life."

Well, getting used to a wardrobe change from business clothes and high heels to cowboy boots and a large assortment of mostly blue jeans was challenging, but learning the dialect was another story. (I will tell you more about that later.)

As part of my cowgirl training, Bob told me I had to watch Lonesome Dove, a cowboy cult movie. I couldn't come out of the house for three days until I watched that six-hour movie. It made me realize how tough these people had to be to survive in the country. The change I made from city person to learning how to be a country girl was abrupt, challenging, and occasionally unsettling.

Summary

I now realized I was afraid to be alone in the woods, and since I couldn't find my way back to the farmhouse, I made signs like those in the city. I asked Bob to help me hang them on the trees on the different trails, and although he found it funny, he did it to appease me.

I was not used to the isolation of living on a farm. Since it is located on seven hundred acres, we cannot see our neighbors, and it is so easy to get lost in the woods.

I was used to leading a very active social life in Scottsdale, Arizona, so living in the country was a huge adjustment.

CHAPTER 3

Down Home on the Farm

I was committed to giving Kentucky a try, especially since I wanted to be with Bob. It would mean I would have to come out of my comfort zone a lot and expand my range of what was familiar. I was willing to learn about the culture of the people as well as to learn how to ride the spirited horses. I was about to encounter many foreign situations, but I was willing to overcome my fears and work through them.

I was very social in Scottsdale, so being on a family farm was isolating for me at first, but I later learned that this has its advantages as well. Something is very peaceful about lush, green rolling hills and no traffic or pollution, not to mention no fashion police.

When I first saw the house at Smokey Valley Farm, I was in total awe at its uniqueness and beauty. Bob's grandparents had bought this house as a kit from a Sears and Roebuck catalog, and it was delivered to town by train, and then hauled by a mule-drawn wagon to this lot and constructed in 1907. The farmhouse is a turn-of-the-century Victorian-style home that has a fabulous back porch with a porch swing and rockers that have seen many family gatherings over the years. Both Bob and his dad were born in the bedroom where we now sleep.

Bob is a seventh-generation Kentuckian and is proud of his heritage and this rugged lifestyle in eastern Kentucky he has come to know. Bob has preserved this lovely home and its memories and added an addition to the original home to make it bigger. He also put a big patio around back where we enjoy having meals and watching the horses run across the creek in the pasture. Across the street is a thirty-stall barn with a riding ring, round pen, and automatic walker, as well as a working office for the barn manager. I like to sit in a gazebo in the riding ring and watch Bob work the horses.

Bob came from a loving family with good values and strong work ethics. It was his quest for knowledge and his passion for reading that earned his scholarship to continue his education, and he ended up with a PhD. After he finished school and went off into the world to become a CEO at age twenty-nine, he learned about society, fine dining, and the other things that the world beyond Smokey Valley Farm had to offer.

He spent years traveling and working hard, and now, years later, he shares his passion for horses, as well as his country lifestyle, with me.

I am truly blessed to have met such a smart man with such a big heart and the patience to teach me about his world.

I learned many things about living on a horse farm in a relatively short time. I was not used to so much physical labor and eating dinner so late, not to mention the unexpected excitement when a horse or cow would get loose and neighbors or people driving by would knock on the front door to tell us a cow was in the road. I really liked seeing all the wildlife, such as deer and wild turkeys, and goats, donkeys, and mules. Before, I had seen these animals only in a zoo. I learned about mules, the offspring of horses bred to donkeys. They cannot reproduce, but they are great to ride.

I couldn't believe how much Bob knows about horses. He is like a modern-day John Wayne, for Bob wears spurs and a cowboy hat and carries a holster with a gun and a knife.

Bob breeds and raises Tennessee Walking Horses on the farm. We currently have a head count of fifty-six horses, two ponies, and about fifty black Angus beef cattle. At first, I didn't know how to tell him I was not a big meat eater and that I preferred chicken. He said that he used to raise chickens, but they were too messy. I saw how horses were bred, as well as artificial insemination. Watching colts being born at the farm is always a special time, and it is enjoyable to see them stand up for the first time with their long spiderlike legs.

Photo taken by Emily Aadland

I'd never heard about Tennessee Walking horses until I came to Smokey Valley Farm. I learned about their smooth ride and fast gait. I also learned a horse is worried about only three things: food, rest, and survival.

We had one Missouri Fox Trotter horse in the barn named Foxy. Bob gave Foxy to me as my first horse. She tended to spook if approached from behind, and she was always a bit nervous. When I first started riding Foxy, she was very sensitive because she had been abused by a previous owner, so I had to be very cautious with her. One day when we were with a group of other riders, Bob told me to show her who the boss was and to use my new spurs, for she was not listening to my commands. So I did what he said, and she exploded like a bronco rodeo horse. She reared up, then bucked, and then went from side to side. Foxy did this whole routine at least twice. Finally, I flew off like a lawn dart to the left, and there I sat in a puddle of mud with one boot on and the other one still in the stirrup. At that point I was not happy about my first fall or with her, so Bob helped me up, we traded horses, and we continued on.

We enjoy group rides with neighbors and friends throughout the area, where wonderful trails are in the woods. Carter Caves State Resort Park has endless trails in beautiful hill country. I don't mind riding when the weather is pleasant, but when the trails get muddy, they become more challenging to ride.

Along with getting familiar with the trails, my nervous horse, and the neighbors, I was also busy getting the farmhouse in order and learning where things were and how to operate things. I had never driven a four-wheeler before, so there were so many firsts here with Bob on the farm.

The property on which the farmhouse stands includes a thirty-stall barn, a round pen, a riding ring, a cabin on a lake, and a chapel. We recently had our first wedding at our chapel at Smokey Valley Farm, and it was so quaint and romantic. That was where Bob wanted us to get married. We've had celebrities inquire about weddings there as well, for this chapel is hidden in the woods. It is a great place to get away from the media.

There is a full working office for Bob where he does his other passion, which is mentoring CEOs and start-up medical companies. Ann, our assistant, runs the office and makes sure things go smoothly, and she is very flexible with all the changes that come her way.

Golda, Bob's mother, lives in a house at the end of our driveway, and she is wonderful and amazing for being eighty-four years of age. She is a true mountain woman, healthy and strong; she can cook just about anything, and she knows how to survive in the wilderness with basic supplies. Golda is my mentor and taught me about country cooking, as well as about gardening and canning goods for the winter months.

One day I saw Golda on the top of the hill by the barn. She had a basket on her arm, and when I told her she should get down before she fell down, she just laughed at me and told me she was hunting for morel mushrooms. She taught me about morel mushrooms, which she picks each spring in the woods. She puts her special batter on them and fries them . . . and wow, are they delicious! She never acts her age and amazes me with all that she does. She taught me how to pick berries, and, believe me, there is an art to doing that without getting all scratched up. She also taught me how to climb fences, which is something I never had to do before. That was very entertaining, for I got stuck and she had to help me off the fence. She taught me how to make biscuits and gravy, Bob's favorite breakfast.

Speaking of breakfast . . . one morning we had quite the laugh over pancakes. We entertain a lot at the farmhouse, and people come to visit us from all over the United States. Like myself, these people are unfamiliar to the environment in this part of the country. One time a friend was visiting from California. I made pancakes that morning and told him about some pure maple syrup we had from Vermont in a fancy leaf-shaped bottle. He'd be the first to use it. I served him his pancakes and gave him the fancy bottle of syrup, which touted it was pure maple syrup. And I just assumed it was supposed to be clear instead of the usual brown color. Well, when I went back to the stove, the next thing I heard was, "Good God, Jane. Are you trying to kill me?" And then he broke out in laughter. I had no idea what he was talking about, and I was awestruck and walked to the kitchen table. He then said, "This is not syrup."

Now Bob's curiosity was piqued. He grabbed the bottle, smelled it, and laughed. Bob said, "So that's where my moonshine went." I later learned Bob had a tendency to fill empty jars with moonshine and didn't mark them or tell anyone, including me. To this day we still laugh about moonshine syrup.

This Thing Called Moonshine

For the most part, moonshine is a clear alcohol, a liquid made by the locals for the locals. Making it is a way of getting around the dry county laws. We live in an area with a large population of Baptists, and many people consider drinking alcohol to be sinful. So I guess the politicians figure that if they make it illegal to sell alcohol, no one will drink. Boy, have they got that all wrong!

Getting back to the farmhouse . . . a creek runs behind the farmhouse, and we drive our vehicles through it. I was so excited when I drove the Hummer across the creek for the first time, for it was a big deal for me to drive off-road that first time. Bob encouraged me and talked me through the whole thing, and I was glad I did it. Coming from a city, you don't have this opportunity very often.

Some trails in the area are more challenging than others. The limestone rocks in eastern Kentucky can be slippery, and when it rains the trails get even slicker. I've found that the trick is to not get all of your horse's hooves on the same rock all at once and to cross on a vertical path over the rock.

On one ride, I led most of the way on a mare named Dusty, and things were going smoothly until I hit a patch of mud. It was almost like I stepped in quicksand. Before I knew what happened, my horse was up to her knees in this large puddle, and I did a somersault headfirst over the top of her head and hit the ground rather hard. Boy, did that smart! I had taken her bridle completely off, and luckily she stood there and looked at me until someone was able to grab her. I'm amazed and grateful that I lived to talk about this and that I wasn't paralyzed or trampled by my horse.

Bob came over and said, "Move your head to the right," and he turned my head to the right. Then he said, "Move your head to the left," and he moved my head to the left. Then he said, "You're fine, so get back up on your horse." I decided to back off on riding the horses for about a week after that episode.

After about a week, I started riding again. This time we were on a narrow trail, and we had tried a tie down for my horse, and for some reason she didn't like it. A tie down is a piece of leather from the chin strap to the girth that keeps the horse from throwing her head up. We were on the edge of a cliff, and she refused to go forward. She was going backward, even closer to the edge. I knew that horses cannot see their back feet, so I had to dismount from the opposite side rather quickly. I no longer felt safe or wanted to get back on that horse, so I looked at Bob and said, "Call me a cab, for I want to go home."

Bob tried really hard not to laugh in my face, because he knew I was upset. So he looked at me and said, "Honey, you are in the middle of the woods, and there are no cabs here." He looked at his horse and said, "This is your cab. The only way home is to ride my horse, and I will take yours."

I was hesitant to accept his offer, but I knew his horse was gentle, so I agreed and made it home safely from another day of adventure with Bob.

Despite my challenges with the different horses, as well as with mastering my balance after my shoulder surgery, I never quit. I kept on trying to improve my riding skills and knowledge of this new world.

It is such a wonderful feeling to get up in the morning and hear the horses right outside your door and to see them play and buck.

I also learned horses can get bored, so sometimes they play with a rubber ball with a handle on it. They can pick it up with their mouth and toss it.

One week I observed how to castrate calves. This is something not to attempt alone!

Although I had many new learning experiences, one that was a bit scary was herding cattle. Every year we pick out the best cow to supply our meat for the following year. We take it to some Amish people, and they cut and pack up the meat after it is cured.

Once we had two baby colts born on the same day. It is always so amazing to see their long legs and to watch them wobble and then stand for the first time.

The nearby town of Olive Hill is very small, with a population of two thousand. It is like something out of an old western movie. In the past, this town thrived from clay mining and fire brick manufacturing businesses, but since the businesses shut down, the town has never recovered. This was a place where people never locked their doors or took their keys out of their vehicles when they were home. Entertainment consisted of going to the Dairy Queen or to the one and only restaurant, called Walkers. Summer horse shows were events where you could see all the neighbors you hadn't seen all winter.

In the country, kids grow up a lot differently from the way they do in the city. Since activities are not abundant like they are in the city, kids make up their own fun. I found the kids in the country are more mature and take things on at earlier ages, whereas in the city we still nurture our young. When I was growing up in New York City, I was not allowed to get dirty and would be punished if I even got a little mud on my shoes.

In the country, children are called young'uns, and they are free to roam about the country and ride horses, use a pocket knife, and shoot guns. I met the most amazing four-year-old named Mose Oppenheimer. He wasn't afraid to get on a horse a lot bigger than him, and he'd even use a whip to make it go faster. Mose was not your average four-year-old. His grandfather, who is also named Mose, taught Bob how to be a cowboy and shared his love of horses. Bob loves sharing his knowledge with young cowboys in training, and we both get delight from watching young Mose grow and acquire new knowledge. Little Mose has his own pocket knife, and he uses it to whittle twigs, 'cause that's what country boys do to pass the time.

Then there is Wyatt Sullivan, new to the cowboy scene, who visited his grandparents down the road. We did pony rides for his birthday party.

This is Joey Sciacca, just hanging out around the barn.

Then there are cowgirls in training as well, like Joey's sister Sienna.

I learned that things on the farm have a specific purpose, and this is a simpler life where people are challenged for the basics in life, so designer things don't matter at all like they do in other places. This was the ultimate experience, for it was so liberating to not be encumbered with "stuff." I've found that I can enjoy life more than anything. Living a simpler life makes things less important and people more important.

The first time I went to Walkers, the only restaurant in town, I couldn't believe that practically everything on the menu was fried. The prices were so low that it was like going back in time. I was used to eating healthy and eating mostly fish. Nutrition is a bit of a challenge here. Many times I've thought about writing a letter to Oprah, because she had a special show about people in the Midwest who have a high incidence of obesity from eating too much fried food. I learned that everything was cooked in bacon grease to give it flavor.

The people are very friendly and down to earth here and will do anything to help you. Once I called a wrong number on the phone and ended up spending a half hour talking to a sweet woman who said she would get out her phone book and look up the correct number for me. It was a switch to have someone on the other end so eager to help me reach the correct number instead of hanging up.

As I was adapting to my new farm life, I realized how much hard work it is. Every year we had to get rid of the telltale signs of winter. I planted flowers and an herb garden and was quite proud of myself for my success with those projects. We had a major landscaping cleanup project, so I helped with trimming trees and bushes around the farmhouse. We hung up birdhouses after filling them with seed.

The state bird is the cardinal, and their colors are so vivid. My favorite bird is the hummingbird, for it is amazing that they flap their wings so many times a minute that it makes their wings almost invisible.

Another form of entertainment we do at the farm is cowboy mounted shooting.

Chris Coleman

This is something not to be tried by a novice rider or after a sip of moonshine. It takes a very calm horse, a horse who is not affected by the sounds of gunshots. The horse's speed and coordination are also important.

Not all of our horses like having a gun fired by a rider on their back, so I keep earplugs on hand for the horses as well as for our guests so that the noise won't be as loud. The coordination factor comes into play while the rider holds on with one hand and rides a horse around a balloon obstacle course. Timing is also important as riders go through the course, aim, hold, and fire a gun to burst the balloons—all while hoping to make good time. This game can be quite entertaining, because so many factors come into play, such as wind moving the balloons or horses being spooked by the balloons. Riders also have to pay attention and hold their arm straight out to the side so they don't fire the gun toward their horse's ear. They have to concentrate so that they don't miss a balloon because of bad aim or a spooked horse . . . you get the idea. In the end, the winner is the person who gets the most balloons and makes the best time getting through the obstacle course.

Living with Bob is like being in a James Bond movie. It's high adventure and action-packed, and you never know what will happen next. One day in the early spring, Bob was eager to take Max, his 1997 911 turbo Porsche, for a drive, since it had been in the garage all winter long. I had already made plans for the day, so I told him to go ahead and take a drive and have a wonderful day. Max was a collector's car, and he had his own garage. Only four hundred of these cars were made in the United States. Not to mention it, but he was wicked fast!

Bob's '55 Chevy

(Max) the porsche is in the middle.

When I didn't hear from Bob by dinnertime, I started to worry. About an hour later I received a call from Bob. He said, "Honey, I am sitting at the edge of the road watching Max burn."

I couldn't believe what I was hearing. I said, "Honey, are you okay?" I asked, "What happened?"

Bob said he had been driving down the road. Suddenly, he happened to look in the rearview mirror and saw smoke. He was driving out in the country in a fairly remote area, but he got out. As he was getting out of the car, he noticed the tires were on fire. Well, that really got his attention, so he ran away from the car as fast as he could. Within minutes the car blew up—not once, but twice.

This is what Max looked like after the fire.

A house was down the road, and with nothing else to do, Bob started walking toward that house to see if anyone was home, for it was a Sunday afternoon. Luckily for him, someone answered the door. It was too late to do anything for Max, for he was totally burned to a crisp, so the gentleman offered Bob a ride home to our farmhouse.

Needless to say, Bob needed some alone time to grieve the loss of Max, plus recover from the shock of almost losing his life and the reality of the close call he had just had. I contacted his friend Steve, and he came over with dinner and a bottle of wine that helped ease the pain.

We later found out that Bob had never been notified of a recall, and the fire had something to do with transmission fluid leaking onto the engine. I'm just glad I still have my Bob, for a car can always be replaced!

They say things happen in threes. Well, I do believe there is some truth to that, and the next week proved it. We drive a Polaris, (an all-terrain vehicle), on the farm. Since the weather was getting warmer, I wanted to take out the removable windshield for the summer months. The guys that help us around the farm were really busy that week, so they did not have a chance to remove the windshield.

Meanwhile, Bob and Steve set out for an exploration trip on the Polaris to check out a trail that they had never used before. We were planning to take a wagon ride on that trail the next day. They set off on their field trip with a cooler of beer and came back with mud all over the Polaris, mud all over their shoes, and a broken windshield. I asked what had happened, and they said, rather casually, that oh, a tree branch had fallen. Thank goodness that windshield hadn't been removed a few days earlier.

Get ready for number three, for it is a doozy! Bob had gotten into a new hobby, riding horse-drawn wagons, and he wanted to share this passion with his friend Steve. You could say that Steve was in boot camp, for Bob has a tendency to let you sink or swim when it comes to new experiences (so I am learning). This was all new to Steve, so with great excitement, he dove right into learning how to drive a team of horses pulling a wagon. Steve had gotten a wonderful pair of Morgans to pull his wagon. But his wagon wasn't ready the day we were going on the trip, so he used our wagon. We had about fifteen riders who would ride around the wagons on the day trip we were about to take. We brought along plenty of adult beverages to be enjoyed by all, as well as a grill for BBQ and other goodies. Steve's wife, Ann, made a brisket. She is a great cook, so we were looking forward to that as well.

I almost forgot to tell you that we also had two dogs along on the trip, which was not unusual in that part of the world. One of the two dogs was a heeler, a herding dog breed that is trained to bite the back of the feet of horses or cows to get them to move forward.

Everything was going along smoothly, and we made it to our first stop. We stopped for bathroom breaks and refreshments, and Steve thought he would take a little break as well. The only problem was that Steve didn't tell anyone he was leaving. The heeler went to the back of the wagon and started biting the back of the horses' legs to get them to move. Meanwhile, Ann was still in the wagon, waiting for him to come back.

The next thing we knew it was total pandemonium, for things were flying back at us out of the wagon. The wagon took off without a driver, and Ann hung on in the backseat. The guys started running after the wagon to rescue Ann; they told her to jump, and her son-in-law Erin, caught her as the wagon headed for a group of trees. Our friends Joe and Dwight finally grabbed hold of the reins and stopped the runaway wagon. Whew, was that excitement! That was lesson number one: never leave a team of horses unattended.

After the excitement subsided, we moved on and continued on the rocky terrain of Grassy Creek. It was refreshing riding through the creek and splashing water. Once again things were going smoothly. But then, for some reason, Steve decided to take a high road that was normally used by four-wheelers. It was a rather narrow path for a wide wagon, and all I remember was hearing a loud bang as Steve hit the bank of the creek and yelled out, "Ya, boy!" Steve had lawn-darted the wagon into the creek, and this busted the main connection between the front wheels and the rear axle.

So there we were in the wilderness, having to act like MacGyver and being inventive in how to repair this axle with just a few tools at our disposal. Some of the guys rounded up a piece of barbed wire off a nearby fence and used a tree branch to hold the axle together. Surprisingly, that worked, and we were back on our way. We made it to an island to have our cookout lunch. We had a fun time and a wonderful lunch.

After lunch we continued off the creek and onto a wood-covered trail, and there were many mud puddles from all the rain we'd had. It was challenging getting through, for Kentucky mud is very slippery and sometimes can just suck you in. I had switched with a rider in the wagon and was now in the wagon with Ann and Steve. A really big mud hole was coming up, and I was getting nervous, for there was no other way around it. Steve's horses were not ready for all this adventure. They hadn't been used in a while, so they were not conditioned for this particular kind of ride. As we approached the mud puddle, the horses started to lose their footing. They were sliding so much that one of the horses landed sideways, and that's when I realized we were in trouble. Ann and I jumped ship—literally. The other riders on horses came to our rescue and helped to keep us clear of the mud as we jumped out.

Then we stood by and watched as the guys tried to get the horse right side up and guide them both out of this mud hole. We ended up having to unhook the horses and walk them out of the puddle. The wagon was so heavy we used a team from one of the other wagons to get this wagon out of the huge mud hole. It was quite the challenge, but somehow, with great determination, the guys and horses pulled it off.

We were again on our way, and I decided to jump back onto my horse instead of riding in the wagon. Surprisingly, the axle fix held up through all of this, but now it was starting to work its way loose again, so the boys had to do another repair job to keep us moving along. Things were going smoothly for a while again, but then we had to climb a big hill. It was too much hill for the horses; they gave it all they could, but they were too tired. We gave them a rest and water, and we decided it was best to use the other team of horses to get the wagon up the hill. It worked, and we got the wagon up the hill, but then the axle was beyond repair so we decided to leave Steve with the busted wagon, a cooler full of beer, and Bob's knife and gun.

It was getting dark, and we were at least an hour's ride away from our farm. We told Steve we would be back when we could to pick him up. We had to ride through some rugged terrain to get back, and I was very tired from riding all day. It was about 11 p.m. by the time we got back to the barn, put our horses up, and got in the truck and horse trailer to rescue Steve. By the time we got back to Steve, he had a party going on in the middle of the woods with some people who were on four-wheelers. It was about midnight by the time the guys got back to the barn with Steve and the broken wagon. We all had quite the day.

So much for our adventures at the farm. As you can see, every day is action-packed, with much activity. I am so proud of myself, for I am doing so many things I never dreamed I would or could do. Bob has really stretched me out of my city girl comfort zone.

I also started to learn the local language, which is quite different from what I knew. Here are some translations of the country dialect:

A holler is a valley.

Put the squeeze on it means apply pressure.

Young'un means children, and I thought they were asking if I had any onions?

Other Kentucky sayings are:

"I don't care to" means I don't mind. Or okay, I'll do it.

"That's a bad dog" means it's really cool!

"Well, hail" means well, hell.

Dwight is a cowboy friend of Bob, and he always has a new saying when you ask him how he is doing. He will say things like

"If I were any finer, I would be twins."

"Finer then a frog hair split three ways"

"If I were any finer, I'd have to take somethin' for it."

"Finer then a prickly bush"

Well, you kinda get the idea that you never know what he will say next, and it certainly makes you stop and think.

As I mentioned earlier, in Kentucky they fry most of their food or cook it in bacon grease. This was a shock to me, for I like to eat healthy. Vegetables are a foreign entity here. I couldn't believe they fry just about everything, from Snickers bars to vegetables. So eating healthy is definitely a challenge here, and many people are overweight compared to people in other parts of the country.

One time Bob's mom fried some green tomatoes for me, and I had no idea there was such a thing. I thought it was something they made up in a movie, but I have to say I tried it and, to my surprise, it was really good.

Bob's favorite foods are fried chicken and biscuits and gravy. His mom makes a really good blueberry cobbler unlike anything I've ever tasted. Yes, people really enjoy their food here. You don't see many anorexia issues here—quite the opposite.

I am trying to learn how to cook country, for I am a purebred, 100 percent Italian, originally from New York City. When I made my first corn bread, it turned out more like a soufflé. I thought it was good, but Bob said it was too sweet and tasted like cake. Well, at least I tried.

Bob has been giving me the country girl crash course, along with tips for cowgirl attire.

In Kentucky, there is something called "sitting on the stump," which translates to people such as friends and neighbors sitting around talking and sometimes just sitting and saying nothing—just being.

A cabin is also on the property, and a man-made pond is behind it. The cabin is the ultimate man cave, with charm.

It has two bedrooms upstairs. Did I say upstairs?

Actually, there are no stairs. You have to climb a ladder—try doing that after a few cocktails. The bathroom is small, so it is perfect for a quick shower. Just like the farmhouse, the cabin is decorated with antiques that Bob has collected over the years. The man-made pond behind the cabin is turned a brilliant blue each spring with a liquid called Aquashade that they add to the water. In the spring, the days are so much longer here in Kentucky. It is still light out at 9 p.m., so it gives you plenty of daylight to enjoy.

One evening we were at the cabin. The mosquitos started to come out, and I was ready to go back to the farmhouse, but Bob encouraged me to stop and be with nature.

We lay side by side on the dock, and to my amazement, the show began. Bats flew in to eat the mosquitos. We heard deep croaks coming from the bullfrogs from one side of the pond and then the other, and before long all kinds of noises were coming from all around the pond from the different types of frogs and birds. It was nature's symphony. Occasionally lightning bugs would come by. Bob looked at me and said, "This is life—isn't it great?" I smiled back and said yes, knowing he had captured the essence of life here.

I love my cowboy so much. We spend all our time together, and we really enjoy each other's company. And despite our cultural differences, we appreciate each other. We have the true-life fairy tale.

When I witnessed cicada bugs for the first time, they really scared me. They make a loud cricket-type noise and are everywhere. The noise all the male cicadas make when they sing for sex can drown out your own thoughts. I am told they come out once every seventeen years. It's scary to think that I will be sixty-seven years of age the next time they come out. They are ugly, with red eyes and clear wings. They emerge from the ground when the temperature reaches precisely 64°F, and they're looking for just one thing: sex. And they've been waiting a long time. After a few weeks up in the trees, they will die and their offspring will go underground for seventeen years. After they are gone, all that is left is their clear body shell, and quietness is restored to the valley.

There are many colorful plants and flowers here in Kentucky, but I love watching the beautiful colored butterflies surrounding them most of all.

I started making signs for the different trails on the farm, for we are talking about seven hundred acres. I did not know how to navigate in the woods without getting lost, for it all looked the same to me. I named the trails on the farm after some of Bob's favorite horses. We had the fun project of hanging up all the new signs on the trees along the different trails. We had fun driving around on the Polaris in the woods. I guess the best way to describe the Polaris is that it is similar to a golf cart and that it is the vehicle we drive around the farm, since there is so much walking and different areas on the farm can be far away.

Playing Possum

One day I was up at the cabin with Bob. I went to throw something into the garbage can, and to my surprise, I saw this thing with big jagged teeth and a long pointed nose staring back at me. I dropped the lid to the garbage can and ran as fast as I could the other way, screaming the whole time in sheer panic. Bob was down by the pond fishing and said, "Honey, what's wrong?" It was all I could do to tell him what I had seen, for I'd never seen anything like that before in my whole life.

Again, he looked at me and laughed. Bob looked into the garbage can and said, "That is a possum. He's probably still alive . . . just playing possum on you." He took the garbage can down by the pond and slid the possum out of the garbage can to the water. To my surprise, it was alive. It got up and walked away.

The next time I saw a possum was in our front yard at the farmhouse. I had just let the dogs out, and the possum was by one of the trees. Now I knew that the possum was probably still alive, so I waited until the dogs were finished with their morning run. About five minutes after we got all the dogs into the house, that possum was gone. It is interesting to note that he could have been dead if he had not played possum, for the dogs could have had some fun with him. Now I know all about playing possum.

Understanding animal behavior is another step toward being less afraid. Those jagged teeth can be very intimidating!

Summary

I had never been around hot horses, bears, or cicadas.

I had a fear of mud, and I hated to get dirty. Living on the farm made it impossible to stay clean, and after a while I learned it was okay to get dirty and eventually had fun getting dirty, for it was all new to me.

Do not wear white on the farm.

When I went for walks with Golda around the farm, especially around the chapel, there were always horses or cows loose. I was not used to being around loose cows, and the first time they approached us running I was very scared. I looked at Golda and told her to run, and she said calmly, "We don't have to run; they just think we are bringing them food." Golda taught me how to climb a wood fence, and wouldn't you know it . . . she made it over, and I got stuck on top of it.

CHAPTER 4

─wwoⲟ⳾⳾ow─

Equine Pole Dancing and Other Horse Horse-Training Techniques

When I first went to Smokey Valley Farm, many new colts were being born. It was a challenge to find a rider to start them off, for you never knew what would happen. It was not a very desirable position to fill, because riders could get hurt very easily. We had to come up with an idea to familiarize these colts with their surroundings and yet be safe enough to ride, for they had much spunk. We tried conventional things like putting a plastic bag on the edge of a stick and rubbing it across the back of their head and ears, but somehow that was not enough.

Riders in this part of the country know there are all kinds of distractions, from flying garbage when the wind picks up, to school buses and farm tractors. Not to mention fire, such as when someone is burning trash, or fast-moving cars on these one-lane roads. We had some old telephone poles that the phone company had left behind some years back, so we put one in the ground fairly close to a road. This location was close enough to a road that the horses could hear and see the traffic, but they were totally out of harm's way. A colt was first tied very tightly with a heavy rope close to the pole. After two hours, we gradually increased the length of the rope. It was amazing and beautiful to see the colts dance as traffic went by. One colt in particular was very entertaining. He'd kick backward, toward the traffic on the road. Of course he was too far away to reach anything. We covered it all by the time they were finished on the pole: school buses, trucks, trailers, farm tractors, etc. We continued their training on a daily basis until the colts stopped dancing and were totally calm when the traffic came. Then we knew they were ready and safer to ride.

Keep in mind the roads by the farmhouse are very curvy. When vehicles drove around the bend, it looked to the driver like a horse was in the road. At the beginning we had a few complaints from the neighbors, saying it was cruel to tie a colt up so close to the road. We explained why we were doing this and told them it was for the safety of the rider and to acquaint the colts with most of the common elements that they would be exposed to before we put a rider on their back. Then they started asking us if they could bring their horses down for a session on our magical pole that transformed any horse to be calmer when confronted with traffic.

The Round Pen

Gaining respect and trust is your main goal in the round pen. This is a technique that is usually done before riding a horse, and it's used as well for behavior modification. It allows you to establish a bond of trust between you and your horse. In the wild, horses establish a dominance order, in which the one that is dominant can control the body movements of the other horses. The round pen allows the trainer or rider to establish leadership in the human-to-horse relationship by controlling the horse's motion.

In getting ready to work in the round pen, you definitely want to note your horse's overall demeanor, head position, position of his ears, and where his attention is. You can tell a lot by just watching your horse's ears. If both ears are planted forward, you might as well be a thousand miles away, because they are not paying attention to you. If they occasionally tip their inside (closest) ear toward you, they are starting to listen to you and pay attention. If their ears are pinned back to their neck, look out!

I like to use the KISS (keep it simple, stupid) method to make my horse go forward. The round pen is an excellent place to practice your signals, cues, and directions that you give your horse. We also want the horse to look to us for guidance and leadership. When horses understand what you are asking and are comfortable, they will lick their lips.

Most horses retreat or run from threats or danger. This behavior is called the flight response. Note that I said most horses. My horse Hombre, on the other hand, had no clue about the flight response. He would run through you and over you. Once when he got tired of the games, Hombre decided to jump the eight-foot wall and was hanging on the wall with his front legs over the top. We finally got him down, which was no easy task, and decided he was one horse who was not a good candidate to be round-penned.

In most instances, the horse will eventually respond to the person in the middle, where the sound of a whip snaps, as the dominant figure. When the horse finally trusts you, a bond is created so that when you turn your back and walk away from the horse, it will follow you.

The round pen is a reflection of how you relate to life, and the horses respond to your body language as you approach them as well as when you walk away. This is just like the way people respond to your nonverbal communication in everyday life.

Myler Bit System

A bit or mouthpiece has a great impact on how your horse responds to your commands. Bits can do only two things: cause resistance or cause relaxation. If a horse resists your commands, he's probably trying to tell you that he's uncomfortable with the bit and the pressure it puts on his tongue. Tongue pressure plays an important role in resistance. When a horse is resisting the bit, he's really protesting tongue pressure because the bit is interfering with his ability to swallow.

Bits are designed for different levels of a horse's behavior as well as its experience. This is one of Bob's big secrets in managing horses that are brought to us when owners say they can't control their horse. Bob will do one of two things. He checks to see if the horse has any wolf teeth, which can be very painful when the rider pulls back on the reins, and he looks at the bit the rider is using. If it is the bit, Bob may try another bit to see how the horse responds. Amazingly, switching the bit can make all the difference in the world. The key is knowing which bit to use, and of course Bob knows most of them.

Summary

The round pen is like lessons in life, in that how you approach a horse and how he responds is how other people perceive you in life. You have to convince the horse you are bigger than him and you are the boss. This process teaches you how to deal with confrontation and conflict in life. It is fearsome to some to be enclosed with something bigger than them while not knowing how the horse will respond. Hombre tried to climb the wall and bucked a lot . . . now, that was scary!

CHAPTER 5

———— ⁓⁓⌒⦿⌒⌒⦿⌒⦿⌒⌒⁓⁓ ————

Nantahala River

I t was hard to believe it was already Memorial Day. We were going to visit our friends Roger and Lori at Buck Creek in the Nantahala National Forest in North Carolina. Buck Creek is tucked away deep in the woods. We took three horses with us on this adventure. This was not an ordinary vacation, and I had no idea what I was in for on this weekend trip. Bob said the area would be a good place to test my riding ability in a different environment.

This episode started on Thunderstruck, a windy, narrow road along the Nantahala River. Around Memorial Day, the trees are as green as can be, and your soul gets lost in seeing the beauty of the mountain vistas and watching the river run over the rocks. When Bob told me we had to drive our truck and horse trailer through the river, I really thought he was kidding to see what my reaction would be—but he wasn't! He looked at me and said, "Baby, hang on. We are about to ford the river to cross over to the other side."

As we plunged into the water, I hung on to the door handle for security, not knowing what to expect next. Bob laughed and said that I was white-knuckling the door handle. All I know is that this was the first time I'd ever gone off-road in a vehicle in water that deep. After our rather bumpy ride across the river, we would be on the narrow dirt road again. Yet just as we'd get to the other side, we'd have to negotiate a very sharp turn with a big granite rock, a rock that could do much damage to our truck if we hit it. I guess I failed to mention we had an exceptionally large horse trailer that was really way too big for this narrow dirt road.

Bob lives for adventure, and I always pray we get through it safely. Despite the size of our exceptionally large horse trailer and the high water, we made it across safely. The ride across was rather bumpy, even though we took it slowly. Just as we made it across, we heard a loud bang. Bob got out of the truck to assess what had happened. We'd hit the large granite rock and damaged our fender and a tire, so now we had to change a tire.

After we changed the tire, it was a continuation of the scary ride for me, for we had to go up the side of a mountain on the narrow road with our oversized truck and trailer and pray we didn't go over the edge. The whole way I tried not to look at the drop-off down below on my side of the truck. I told Bob, "The next time we come here, I will take Valium as well as some oxygen to keep me going on this narrow road."

Bob laughed and said, "You need to cowgirl up!"

Finally, after much anticipation and careful navigating to stay on the road, we reached our friends' cabin. It was an amazing cabin our friends had built in a very secluded area with a stream running between their barn and the cabin.

I thought it was amazing that the only way to get across the stream was to walk across a log and hold on to a high wire that they had strung across in between two trees.

Once we had settled in, the guys went fishing and caught trout. We had a fish fry the first night. The next day the guys went riding, but I stayed behind with the Lori and Bonnie, (Rodgers sister) and we went for a walk.

Our friend Roger had a smoker, so he roasted a whole pig for us, which he started at night and cooked well into the next day. It was hard for me to look at it, for I'd never seen a whole roasted pig before.

After dinner Bob had the idea of going for a moonlight ride on our horses. I thought it sounded like a wonderful idea, and although I'd never ridden a horse at night, I was in. I thought it was a good idea until I realized we couldn't see the moon and that it was pitch black outside, except for an occasional lightning bug. Roger told me not to worry, that the horses could see in the dark and to trust the horses. Although this might have been true, I couldn't stop thinking about the drop-off I had seen on the way in, and I hoped my horse would stay on the dirt road.

Bob never ceases to amaze me. Out of his saddlebag he pulled a light that I later learned would clamp onto his baseball cap, so we could see where we were going. The only problem was that every time he turned his head to talk to me, I was blinded by the light on his baseball cap. I finally told him to keep his head straight and not to turn and look at me when he was talking. We both laughed as we made our way through the darkness in the woods. In some parts of the woods, Bob turned off the headlight so that we could see the beauty of the moon beaming through the trees. I was glad when we made it back to the cabin, for it was a new experience for me to ride a horse in the dark.

The next day I went four-wheeling for the first time in my life. We took paths through the woods, and it was so neat to climb the mountain. We stopped when we got to the top and savored the view beneath us. We had a panoramic view of all the mountains in the distance. We had a lot to eat that weekend and many new experiences for me.

The Second Time Around

The following year, we went back to visit our friends Roger and Lori at Buck Creek. We decided to go back with a bigger trailer then we had the first time—all I can say is, who did the math? Somehow, going across the bumpy terrain while crossing the creek seemed easier this time, maybe because I knew what to expect. We cleared the big jagged granite rock that got our tire and fender the last time. We were even doing well navigating the turns on the narrow windy road with our big truck and horse trailer. But as we made the last turn to get into our friends' road, a back tire on the horse trailer went off the road. As I looked down, I gasped, for we were on an eighty-foot drop-off above the creek, and the trailer was sliding backward. Since time was of the essence, I looked at Bob and said, "This isn't good; we need to get out now." So I jumped over the middle console and got out on the driver's side after Bob. I ran for help to get our friends, since this was not a normal situation for AAA and they probably would have never found us. Bob stayed behind and tried to quickly get our horses out of the trailer. With this type of trailer, all of our saddles and gear had to be removed first to get the divider to move so we could get to the horses. Need I say, we didn't have much time to spare?

Meanwhile, I ran down the rocky dirt road in my wedge heels and told our friends what had happened. When they saw the look of panic on my face, Bonnie and Paul and the neighbors Bobby and David, all came immediately for a rescue mission. The horses had to jump to the side where there was land instead of the other side off the cliff, which was a little tricky! We got our horses out safely, and then the trailer started to shift downward again. We took the horses down to the barn and got them settled in. Roger returned in his truck with a rope and winch. The trailer was now holding in position, as it had wedged against a hemlock tree that was about four inches in diameter. The guys chained a pulley to that hemlock, passed the winch cable through it, and then went to the front trailer axle and made a loop, fastening it with a hook so that it wouldn't flip over. Roger then pulled our truck and trailer out with his dually truck, and we were able to get all four wheels back on secure ground.

I was totally amazed at how close we had come to going over the cliff, for I remember looking back as I ran for help. What I'd seen was frightening, with the twisted horse trailer held in place by only one small tree. That small tree kept the trailer from going completely over the edge. We were grateful for the fast response of help, for it could have gotten ugly!

Okay, so now we got settled in ourselves, had a cocktail, and talked about our adventurous entrance. In the back of my mind I hoped that nothing else crazy would happen that weekend. After dinner we called it a day. I was emotionally worn-out from all the excitement.

The next morning we got up and went for a day ride. We rode our horses to a neighborhood picnic. There were many good southern dishes, all freshly cooked. We had an uneventful ride, which I was grateful for.

The following day was a whole different story. Again, we set out for a day ride. All was well until Roger, who was riding in front of me, yelled out, "Snake!" I didn't get too concerned, for I thought it probably was a garden snake. I paused for a minute and looked around. Since I didn't see the snake, I decided to continue. But as I continued, Bob stopped in his tracks. He was following me, so that's when I realized the snake had been coiled up under my horse, and it was not a garden snake! Luckily for me, Hombre did not see the snake. Hombre stepped on the snake two times while it was coiled up. This was definitely a poisonous snake, a black phase timber rattler with nine rattles and one button on his tail.

Bob saw the whole thing, since he was right behind me. All he could say was, "What a beautiful snake." He sat on his horse and watched the four-foot-long black snake slowly uncoil and exit back into the brush off the horse trail. The previous night had been cold, and the snake was trying to warm up in the sunlight. Thank goodness it wasn't totally awake yet. This was quite the story for our lunch break. I was just thankful that my horse did not see the snake and rear up, and that I was saved by this event.

Not that I am superstitious, but have you ever heard that things happen in threes?

It was getting toward the end of our ride for that day, and we had to take an alternative route because some trees were down, blocking our path. On this alternative route, the ground was very soft and boggy, and a log was down across our path. Roger was the first to cross, and he got off his horse and walked it. I thought about the previous snake incident, and I had no intention of getting off my horse to walk through an area where I couldn't see the ground clearly.

Our friend Paul was next to go over the log. He went slowly, and, although it looked tricky, he made it without getting off his horse. So I thought that if Paul could do it, so could I. But as I started into this muddy mess, my horse's feet sank down into the mud. This meant that my horse was now positioned to go over a higher part of the fallen tree, making it all the more challenging to get through. I felt the forward jerk, and I was unable to sit back in the saddle as Hombre attempted to jump the log. His feet sank deeper into the boggy, muddy ground. That's when my face hit the right side of his neck rather hard, and I fell to the ground, fully banging up my left shoulder and back and hitting my head as well. As I hit the ground, Hombre struggled to free his feet from the deep mud. And as he freed his feet, I thought my luck had run out—I thought I was going to die, for I lay there in pain and shock as Hombre jumped right over me. But to my amazement, despite the sticky mud, he didn't even step on me!

All the guys were watching me, and I had to collect myself and see if I had broken anything. At first I thought for sure my nose was broken, for it was throbbing. After I did a system check and inventory of my body, it appeared I hadn't broken anything, but it sure felt like it. I told the guys that I was done trying to kill myself for the day and was glad we were almost back to the cabin. Once again, Bob was behind me and saw the whole fall, another one of my fine moments. When we got back to the cabin, I took a shower and a nap. A week later I found out I had a mild concussion from hitting the ground so hard with my head. After this incident, I knew I was trading in my cowgirl hat and getting a helmet. Later I was nicknamed Bruisy from all the black and blues from this fall.

I had had two miracles in one day. Yes, "Jesus loves me!"

It was an adventurous weekend, and none of my friends could top the events that took place that weekend for me. I was happy to be headed home, but we still had to go over the same narrow windy road we came in on. So the guys followed us until just after the river fording to make sure we made it across safely, and then we said our good-byes. Maybe after that weekend I should have changed my name to Lucky.

Summary

I had a fear of night riding, and I had to learn to trust my horse, in the areas where it was pitch black. I had learned earlier that horses have good night vision, but it was scary at the time. I defied death several times in one day, but kept going. My horse stepped on a poisonous snake two times, and then Hombre unexpectedly jumped a log and I was ejected into the mud.

CHAPTER 6

———∿∿∾∾⊙⊰⊙⊱⊙∾∾∿∿———

There Goes the Bride!

We decided to have our wedding at the chapel at Smokey Valley Farm. We were so happy, and we enjoyed spending most of our time together at the farm.

The morning was cool on October 10, 2009. The leaves were starting to turn colors, and it was drizzling outside. This was our long-awaited wedding day, which took much preparation. For on this day, unlike most, our barn had been converted into a beautiful, romantic dance hall for our rehearsal dinner. Our garage had been miraculously transformed by Bob's sister Shirley (she can do anything) into a master banquet hall. We had everyone involved in the transformation of the barn and garage, and when it was finished it was magnificent. Shirley is very talented. I showed her a picture of how I wanted the rooms to look, and with little or no sleep, she made it happen. She draped tobacco paper across the rafters on the top of the barn.

In case you are not familiar with it (for I wasn't), tobacco paper is bleached white, and it is light enough to use, yet thick enough, to cover an object and stay in place. Everyone was pitching in to help, from hanging lights to washing horses, etc. Lots was going on everywhere you looked.

I was so excited, I had to hold back my tears of joy several times. We had friends in from all over the country, and it was quite a mixture of people. Most of our friends had never been to Kentucky, and they were in for a pleasant surprise.

We wanted our wedding to be different and memorable for all who attended. We started our celebration on the Wednesday before the wedding, which took place on Saturday evening, and we continued celebrating until Monday. We had catered meals for all our out-of-town guests and gave everyone a chance to explore the beautiful countryside and get to know the other guests who attended the wedding and to make new friends. It was kind of a comedy act that week, because almost all of our guests arrived late due to stormy weather and were temporarily separated from their luggage. But by the time the wedding day came around, all had been resolved.

When the photographers arrived on our wedding day to take pictures, we were almost ready. My biggest challenge was to find someone to lace up the back of my dress. Luckily, the female photographer helped me out. Then we were ready for picture taking by our chapel before the guests arrived. Bob was outside waiting for me, and I couldn't help but smile when I looked at him, knowing we would be spending the rest of our lives together.

We rode up to the chapel, and I posed with Shadow, his white stallion. The whole time I hoped Shadow would not try to show off and rear up or do one of his other usual tricks. The only thing Shadow did was eat Bob's boutonniere, so I pulled the biggest rose I could find out of the bouquet I was supposed to throw later at the reception and put it on Bob's tuxedo. After the pictures had been taken, we went back down to the house and waited for the event to begin.

My wedding party and I were picked up outside the back gate of the farmhouse by my team of palomino horses pulling our wagon. A team of mules was pulling the second wagon. We rode to the top of the hill and got into position, waiting for our cue. Bob took off to the barn with the guys to mount their horses and get in position as well. Our guests were shuttled up to the top of the hill to our chapel on the main dirt road. No one knew what to expect or which direction we would be coming from when it was time for our entrance, so the crowd was in total suspense.

All of a sudden a gunshot went off, and everyone looked in all directions, trying to find us and wondering if this was part of the ceremony or if there was reason to be concerned. Little did they know it was Bob who shot the gun. And when he did, we almost lost our best man, Joe, for his horse reared up. Luckily, Joe managed to stay on, so we did not lose our best man. Then all the guys in the wedding party (or as Bob liked to say, his posse) rode down the hill (from a different direction, where the guests came in) to the chapel. The song "Mama, Don't Let Your Babies Grow Up to Be Cowboys" was being played as they rode.

All the guys had on black dusters and black hats, and Bob was wearing a cream-colored parka and hat. I was later told that it was like something out of a wild Western movie. They rode to the chapel, tied up their horses at the posts, and prepared for my arrival. Now that Bob had arrived, our guests were wondering about my entrance. They couldn't figure out which direction I would be coming from, not to mention how I would arrive.

"Pretty Woman" started playing as I went to the chapel in my horse-drawn wagon. And even though it was cold, I kept a smile on my face.

When we were close to the chapel, a photographer popped out from behind a tree and took a flash photo that spooked our horses. It was very scary. My team of horses did a complete turn away from the chapel, almost wrapped the wagon around a tree, and continued to take off at a rather high speed. Luckily we did not hit the big tree we circled, but it was close! I told our little grandbabies, Lizzy and Gracie, in the wagon with me to hold on. They thought it was all part of the ride and loved it. We were very fortunate we had Dwight, a very experienced driver. He turned the team around, and Joey, one of our helpers, grabbed a horse's halter and redirected the team back to the chapel. I couldn't help but think to myself when the horses turned away that maybe Bob thought I had changed my mind.

After the shock of almost hitting the tree and going the other way, I smiled and looked at all my guests and was grateful to arrive at the chapel intact. They assisted me and the grandbabies out of the wagon so the wedding could begin. We had a beautiful private ceremony with our special friends and family in our chapel at Smokey Valley Farm.

Summary

Even though we thought the horses were trained, we didn't even think about the flash of a camera bulb, which could have changed the course of the wedding.

I learned to never let them see you sweat; I smiled as I exited the carriage while quietly thanking God we made it safely.

CHAPTER 7

———〜〜◦◦⊂⟩⊃◦⊂⟩⊃◦⊂⟩◦〜〜———

Westward Ho

Bob bought a dually mega-cab truck, and I had no idea what that was. A dually is a truck with four back wheels. He had to go away on a business trip, and we were getting ready to go on a trip out west. So he asked me to drive the truck to the store and get mud flaps and a stainless steel diamond toolbox for the truck bed. Talk about being out of your comfort zone. I didn't feel anything feminine about this assignment.

I learned that to travel with our animals, the horses had to have a Coggins test and get papers to prove they did not carry any illness.

It gets cold in the winter in Kentucky so we usually head west, and I am not a big fan of being cold, so we spent one winter in Scottsdale, Arizona. We went on margarita rides through the desert and had so much fun. A great Mexican restaurant was about a one-hour ride from where we boarded our horses, and we would ride there for lunch and have margaritas by the pitcher. We learned that although there were very strict laws about drinking and driving in Scottsdale, there was no law about drinking and riding a horse. We were careful and enjoyed our rides home.

One time it was getting late in the afternoon, and we were losing daylight. I was getting worried because we couldn't find our trail to get home, and we passed an area that was highly populated with rattlesnakes. We kept going and finally found our path just as the sun set. It gets really cool in the desert at night, and I had on a sleeveless blouse, so I was so glad to load up our horses into the trailer and go home that night.

One summer day we left the familiar in Kentucky and headed to the unknown (for me). "Westward ho," as Bob would say. Again, Bob told me to be brave and bold and to replace my fears with knowledge, skills, and experience.

We needed two people to load our horses that morning, since we used a two-horse trailer, and the horses we chose to take on this trip were not familiar with loading in it. I had to lead the horses into the horse trailer, and Bob applied pressure to their back end to encourage them to go forward. My horse Hombre is all black, and he is all of three years old. Bob's horse is Mystic, and he is eight years old. Hombre set a good example in loading into the horse trailer for Mystic, because he was more confident. This was my first time loading a horse trailer, and I was so proud of myself.

We planned to be out west for five weeks and to cover many states. Most of our travels would be in Montana, and then in Colorado and Wyoming. On the first day, we drove through states I had not been to before, such as Indiana, Illinois, and Missouri—home of the famous Gateway Arch. Westward ho!

In 1803, approximately 210 years ago, Thomas Jefferson asked Meriwether Lewis and William Clark to organize and lead an incredible expedition to explore and map the westernmost parts of the United States. They were the first Americans to witness the incredible sights and cultures along the upper Missouri River and beyond to the Pacific Coast. All of us who seek to experience the magic of the northern Rockies and beyond followed in their footsteps. May the spirit of adventure and learning that inspired them on their epic journey protect us. Long live the rest of us.

Here is a quote from Teddy Roosevelt about heading west: "There were all kinds of things which I was afraid of at first, ranging from grizzly bears to mean horses and gunfighters: but by acting as if I was not afraid, I gradually ceased to be afraid."

Personal Journal, July 29, 2010

This morning Hombre decided he wanted to go up the ramp into the horse trailer sideways not once, but four times. So Bob broke a small limb off a tree and whacked Hombre in the rump. It was amazing to see how quickly he followed me into the trailer.

We had several detours this morning, due to road construction, but eventually we were westward ho again. Today we drove through Kansas—rolling green terrain and the Great Plains, with almost no trees. We passed the Wizard of Oz Museum, which is all I know about Kansas. I discovered a Manhattan in Kansas, of all places! I found it interesting to learn that since Kansas did not have many trees, they carved their fence posts out of stone and called them post rocks. We saw many cows and long-horned steers. Can you imagine just hanging around and eating all the time? (A steer is a castrated bull, in case you didn't know.) Their life is sort of like my Italian family's, because everything revolves around eating.

We arrived at our first bed and breakfast, and the barn is really clean with an indoor/outdoor run. The elderly couple that runs it is Lee and Laura Lee. They've lived in this quaint old farmhouse in Colorado over thirty years. After we got the horses settled, we decided to have dinner in nearby Fort Collins, Colorado instead of driving to Cheyenne, Wyoming and it was a lovely little town.

Personal Journal, July 30, 2010

We had an action-packed day today. We drove to Cheyenne, Wyoming for Frontier Days. I went to my first rodeo and saw many wild horses and bulls. It was a full day of rodeo activities.

We met our friends Tim and Irene from Boston at the rodeo. They go every year. I think the most action-packed event was watching the cowboys attempt to mount the wild horses and then race them. It was total pandemonium as we watched horses rear up and buck, and one cowboy was dragged on the ground behind his horse.

We had dinner with our friends from Boston, and then we returned to the stadium where the rodeo had been held earlier. A new band named Sugarland was playing in concert. We had never heard of the group before, but we thought they were great. We really enjoyed the concert even though it was a struggle for us to stay awake, since we were still on East Coast time.

Personal Journal, July 31, 2010

We're leaving Cheyenne and driving through Wyoming toward Yellowstone National Park to get to Montana. We will stay at a working ranch in a town called Absarokee for eight days. Dan and Emily Adland are the owners of this original ranch house, which has been in their family since 1893. They breed Tennessee Walkers just like us, as well as gaited mules. Dan is a published author of riding stories, as well as newly published books about Teddy Roosevelt and his time spent in Montana as a young man.

Along the drive we saw many rim rocks, which are rocks along the tops of the bluffs. The Indians used to kill buffalo by chasing them to the top of these rims, and then the buffalo would fall to their deaths. We saw many antelopes roaming the wide open plains. We drove through an Indian reservation and saw teepees on the Wind River Indian Reservation between Shoshoni and Thermopolis. While we were in Wyoming, we drove through rock canyons with spectacular views and several tunnels carved through the rock.

When we finally arrived at our destination in Absarokee, it was pouring rain. We were in the middle of a violent thunderstorm, one with lightning like I have never seen. We sat in the truck and waited and waited in hopes it would let up so we could unload the horses. When the lightning finally let up, even though it was still raining hard, we got out of our dually, unloaded our horses, and took care in getting them settled in after our long journey across the states. When the rain finally stopped, we had a gorgeous rainbow surrounding us. It was so big I couldn't get the whole rainbow when I took the picture. The next week I saw two double rainbows from beginning to end, which is something I have never seen before.

This working farm in Absarokee had a quaint old farmhouse where we would stay. After we unpacked and got the horses settled in for the night, we went to a local restaurant for dinner and then called it a night.

Personal Journal, August 1, 2010

Today was all about getting acclimated to the high altitude and getting food supplies for the week. We went to Red Lodge, the closest town, for our groceries. It was just like the old days, as the town was a good forty-five-minute drive away. The drive to and from town was very scenic, with rolling hills, mountains, and farmlands all mixed together. Later in the afternoon we took our first ride on the farm. Bob says I am a snake charmer, for I rode over another snake today. Luckily this was not a rattler, just a bull snake.

As we were climbing in altitude, the winds started to pick up, and the next thing we knew we were in the middle of violent lightning again. With the winds picking up so strong, I could barely keep my hat on. I turned to Bob and said, "We need to turn around and get to lower ground." He quickly agreed, and we turned around and headed back down to safety. The clouds were moving so fast it was like out of a movie, for the next moment the scene changed.

The air was calm, and the sun was shining again. Yet we thought it was best to stay on low ground for now. We saw many deer running around us as we rode. After our ride we decided to have our dinner at the farmhouse. Bob made quail on the grill steamed with butter and wine, along with grilled bok choy and sautéed potatoes and onions—it was simply wonderful. We washed it down with a good chardonnay.

Personal Journal, August 2, 2010

My union with Bob—well, putting it politely, he's a handful!

There is not much down time and nothing boring with him. He lives each day to the fullest and then some. Let's just say he is aggressively inquisitive and seeks calculated, high-risk adventure. Today we took a wrong turn while looking for a trail, and before we knew it, we were on this narrow windy road going up at a rather high elevation. Our GPS couldn't even pick up where we were. I begged for him to turn around, but there was nowhere to turn around. So, horse trailer and all, we continued to go higher and higher up the mountain. At this time I was white-knuckling the door handle and feeling queasy from the altitude.

We finally found a wide spot in the road, and I was thrilled to know we could turn around and go back and look for the trail we were supposed to go on. Instead, Bob said, "Okay, this is it. Are you ready to ride?"

I was now hyperventilating because of the altitude, as well as the fear of riding on the edge of this very high mountain. I told him that he was crazy and that I had to think it over. Then I decided to cowgirl up and said, "What the heck, we are already up the side of the mountain." We got our horses out of the trailer and rode the rest of the way to the top. In the distance we saw snow-capped mountains.

Granite Peak, Montana

We even saw the forest ranger station and found out later we were on a forest service trail. We also saw the site of an old mining station. We later found out after looking at a map that we were 12,800 feet above sea level—the highest point in Montana, to be exact! It is called Granite Peak, and it's in the Beartooth Mountains. The views were truly incredible and breathtaking, but boy, was I glad to come down off that mountain. What an emotional ride!

The Absaroka Mountains were named after the Crow Indians, who inhabited much of south-central Montana before European settlement. Absaroka is a Crow Indian word for crow. The Beartooth Mountains were named after their resemblance to the jaws of a bear.

What Is Wilderness?

Wilderness is a very special place that is managed in a very special way. Wilderness is a place where the imprint of humans is substantially unnoticed. It is where natural processes are the primary influences and human activity is limited to primitive recreation and minimum tools. This allows one to experience wild places without intention to disturb or destroy natural processes. Change will occur primarily through natural disturbance with minimum human influence.

Lions, Tigers, and Bears?

Did you know there is such a thing as bear pepper spray?

I think it is ironic that it states it should be used to deter charging or attacking bears. Personally, I hope not to be around to experience either! It reads on to say for backup, consider carrying two cans of bear spray, in case you are charged by more than one bear, have more than one incident, or to compensate for wind . . .

Several bear attacks have occurred since we were out west. One of the campgrounds mentioned in reports was outside Yellowstone National Park, a place where we took some day trips. According to the reports, no one knew why a bear attacked the camping area, since there were ample natural food supplies. These were all nighttime attacks at the Soda Butte Campground outside Cooke City. The sow (mama bear) was euthanized, and three cubs were moved to ZooMontana in Billings. These attacks were the most brazen in the Yellowstone area since the 1980s, stirring speculation that the bear suffered some physical ailment or was driven to desperation by tight food supplies.

Did you know grizzlies live more than twenty years?

All I can say is, I am not sticking around to be a "predatory event." I always thought bears ate berries and nuts.

Do you know what a bear jam is? It is a traffic jam caused by the presence of bears.

I learned the differences between a black bear and a grizzly bear. Black bears are generally smaller then grizzlies and have much narrower faces. Weighing around two hundred to four hundred pounds, black bears have shorter, more curved claws than grizzlies do, which help them climb trees.

Grizzly bears are the largest carnivores in the continental United States. They have a distinctive hump of muscle over their shoulders and a wide face. Their fur ranges in color from blond to black, but tends to have silver or grizzled tips, hence the bear's name. Adults average 350 pounds, although some bears have weighed more than 650 pounds.

Bear Clues

To detect the presence of bears, look for signs such as overturned or torn-apart logs, excavated mammal burrows, broken branches and twigs, and claw marks on trees. You may also see scat (droppings) or tracks. Black bear and grizzly tracks are primarily distinguished by their size: grizzly tracks can be more than ten inches long.

Some experts say we should make noise or sing when traveling in bear habitat, so bears won't be surprised by our presence. I was given a set of bear bells to put around my horse's neck by our friend Roger. At first I thought he was kidding, but it turns out they do make sufficient noise. If you spot a bear, experts say do not approach it. Well, I could have told you that one! Moving closer to the bear may provoke a charge or attack. So who is getting close? Female bears with cubs or bears defending a carcass are especially dangerous.

One day while Bob was riding the Stillwater Canyon, in Montana, he spotted a grizzly bear cub not too far away. He turned to his friend John, whom he was riding with, and said, "I don't think we want to stick around and meet the rest of the family." Then they slowly departed in the other direction.

The key factor in a bear encounter is not to make abrupt moves. Bears are hunters and instinctively chase anything that flees. A bear may bluff charge and stop short of touching you. If possible, stay still until the bear calms down, and then slowly back away. If you cannot take a detour, wait until the bear moves away from your route. If the bear knocks you down, curl into a ball and protect your stomach and head and neck.

As a precaution, we carried bear spray and had it readily available if we needed it.

Personal Journal, August 4, 2010

Today we were awakened by a very loud repetitive knock on the door at about 6:30 a.m. When I answered the door, still in my pajamas, it was Dan, the owner of the ranch where we were staying. Dan said our horses had gotten out during the night and that something rather large, like a bear, had come through and scared them enough to kung fu the strong metal gate down. He had gotten a call from a neighbor down the road that some strange horses had showed up at their ranch and had many cuts on their legs. We got dressed without delay and headed out the door. We grabbed a couple of lead lines and got into our truck to go over to the neighbors' house.

When we arrived we saw our horses and were so relieved. Mystic had many cuts on his legs from the metal gate, and a wire fence he had run through. He had broken through the neighbor's wire fence, maybe still shaken up about the bear. The cuts on Mystic's legs were superficial, and in his groin area they were deeper. Hombre had a few scrapes on his side and front leg. He was very happy to see us and told us so by nuzzling close. They'd had a very scary night. We will let them rest and heal up the next few days.

It appeared that something came into their corral at about 3:00 a.m. and spooked them badly enough to make them kick down the corral gate and run. I can't believe we slept through the whole event, which took place right outside our bedroom window—just a few feet away.

The neighbors were less cordial. They were more concerned about the damages to their wire fence than the damages done to our horses. We tied both of the horses to the back of our truck and took them back to the Aadlan Ranch; then we doctored up our horses and fed them.

We realized after all was settled that we were supposed to go to the airport this morning to pick up our son, "Chris", who is flying into Bozeman, Montana, to be with us for a few days, and we then realized we would be a little late in getting to the airport. After the crazy morning that we had, we finally got on the road to go to the airport. As we were driving, we received a call from Chris. We looked at each other before we answered the phone and knew we would have to tell him it would be a few hours before we would get to the airport to pick him up. We were all ready to apologize for being late, only to find out he wasn't coming in until 11 p.m. that night instead of 11 a.m. like we thought. So we had the whole day to spend in Bozeman. We walked around, had some lunch there, and then decided to take a drive to Big Sky to find a place for our horses to stay, for when we would be visiting friends in a few days in Big Sky.

We found a place for our horses and again heard more bear stories. One in particular was about a trail guide who went back on a trail to pick up a pair of sunglasses. As she got off her horse to pick them up, a bear approached her. She immediately dropped to the ground and went into the fetal position, for the bears will not bother you if you are not fighting back. In the meantime she was waiting for an opportunity to reach for her bear spray, which was out of reach on her belt. Finally, as the bear was walking around her, she was able to reach for her spray, and the bear decided to take off and leave her alone.

By now I had heard enough bear stories, and the last thing I wanted to do was go back to the ranch where we were staying and have the strong possibility of seeing a bear. After all, I am a city girl and totally out of my comfort zone!

It was around 7 p.m., and we were still in Big Sky, Montana. We thought we would have a light dinner before we headed to the airport to pick up Chris. All of a sudden I heard my name called in the distance. I turned and it was our friend Kate and two other girls I had not met yet. We were planning to stay with them the following weekend when we came back to Big Sky. Kate introduced me to Ellen and Irene, the twin sisters of Kate's husband. They had just arrived in Big Sky and had come to town to get a bite to eat and to get some groceries. We told them about our bear scare and other adventures. The girls said they were going to the spa the next day and invited me to go with them. Knowing Bob was going to go horseback riding in a heavily populated grizzly bear area near Yellowstone the next day, I quickly decided this was a great option, even though I had nothing with me but the clothes on my back. The girls quickly reminded me I didn't need anything to go to the spa, so in an instant life was feeling familiar and safe again. Bob said he would be back to pick me up the next night, and I kissed him good-bye before he drove to the airport to pick up Chris.

Personal Journal, August 5, 2010

I woke up around 8 a.m. feeling rested and grateful for a good night of sleep. I looked at my cell phone to realize there is no cell service where we were, and then just wondered how Bob and Chris made out with their early morning ride through grizzly country. I then started thinking about the day and looking forward to a girls' day at the spa and regrouping and getting in touch with my feminine side after all the ruggedness I'd endured the days before.

We went to the spa in Big Sky, Montana—or shall I say, me and my angels who rescued me from the grizzly bear ride in Yellowstone. Things were going smoothly at the spa, and I was feeling relaxed now. In between treatments, I decided to go out by the pool and see what the weather was like. I stepped outside, went by the pool, and sat in a chair. As I looked straight ahead, what do you think I saw? In plain view, about three hundred yards away from where I was, a black bear was looking at me as I looked in total disbelief at him. At first I couldn't believe my eyes, and then I was stunned. I remembered what Bob had told me—to back up slowly. So I did.

I thought to myself that Bob would never believe this one. Once I backed away to a safe location, I remembered I had a camera on my cell phone in my pocket, so I pulled it out and snapped a picture. Once I took my picture I was fascinated and amazed while watching the bear. At that moment I overcame my fear and realized that the bear wasn't really interested in having me for lunch. I went back inside feeling rather proud of myself for not running away, but for being a curious onlooker. Some experts say perfume attracts bears. Maybe he smelled all the oils from my massage?

Later that night, Bob picked me up. We went back to the Aadlan ranch house, where we were scheduled to ride with the Aadlans the next day. Our horses' legs were healing nicely from our bear scare, and they seemed up for the ride.

Bob told me on our drive back from Big Sky that while I was AWOL at the spa, they'd decided to go for a ride around the Aadlan ranch instead of driving back to Cody for the early morning ride that they'd originally planned. Before they saddled up for their ride they needed to get a new shoe for Mystic. Thats another story, tell you in a minute.

We had previously negotiated the settlement for the damages done to the neighbors' fence. We were granted the privilege of paying the grand total of $225 for refastening one hundred feet of wire fence and replacing a six-foot long, four-inch brace post that had broken.

My estimate was that it would cost $30 in material and one hour of labor, totaling about $50 at most. Yet it was well worth the money to pay off the neighbors to avoid any more conflict.

Mystic was missing a shoe, which was loosened during his great escape. We were fortunate to find the missing shoe, but now we had no one immediately available to nail the shoe back onto his foot. Bob launched a search for a local farrier. Since he couldn't find one, he thought he would put an easy boot on Mystic and go for a ride on the farm. Just as Bob and Chris were getting ready to take off for their ride, an old dark blue Ford truck pulled into the driveway next to the corral. As the door opened, a Montana cowboy wearing a big floppy hat stepped out of the truck. Bob and Chris introduced themselves to Pedar, the farrier, and quickly discovered Pedar had heard about our situation with the neighbor from hell. Since he was driving by anyway, he thought he would stop by to help replace Mystic's shoe. As it turns out, the shoe replacement merely provided the opportunity to discover that Pedar has an absolute gift for stringing together nearly endless displays of cowboy profanity. He immediately continued to describe in graphic detail the bitch from hell with whom we'd had our encounter during the great horse escape. He also applied his talents in description to anything we wanted to know about, including trails.

The most telling thing about the character Pedar and our newfound friends the Aadlans were their statements that they genuinely hoped that the behavior and animosity displayed by the newly imported neighbors was not even remotely typical of people from Montana. Pedar, the itinerant cowboy/horseshoer who earned a living doing anything he could get paid for, quietly and simply refused to get paid for replacing Mystic's shoe. His refusal to be paid was his way of saying he was embarrassed by the neighbors' behavior and making a bad situation right.

Personal Journal, August 6, 2010

We went for a ride with the Aadlans on one of their favorite trails. We had lunch by a waterfall and tied our horses up to trees on the hills nearby. It was a burnout area that had recently been set on fire by a lightning hit. Even though the trees were burned, there was still beauty to behold as the forest was coming back to life. It was a peaceful ride and, happy to report, we had no bear incidents.

The next weekend we went to visit our friends in Big Sky. After all our wilderness adventures, it was a relaxing and fun time in a more normal environment. I can certainly say I see how they get the name Big Sky, for it seems like the sky is so big compared to the land. Bob went for a ride with his friend Ed and got into a hailstorm. We kept the horses at the 320 Ranch outside Yellowstone. We would definitely keep our horses here again, for it was a clean place with good trails.

I had never been to Yellowstone, so when we left Big Sky we were going to drive through the national park. We tried to enter the park through the northwest corner and met up with a drill sergeant—type woman who was giving us nothing but grief. She told us they needed to inspect our horse trailer if we were to go through the park. She continued on to tell us the rules and that we had to have a wheat-free environment. This meant no bales of hay in the trailer as well as in with the horses, and we had both. She continued on to tell us that in order to do this inspection, we would have to turn around and go back out of the park, then go someplace where we could clean out the trailer of all hay, which meant unloading the horses and much physical labor, not to mention time. Then she said we would have to get a receipt to prove we did what she said. Bob and I just looked at each other, knowing this would take at least a couple of hours. Since we were pressed for time and did not want to throw out our bales of hay, we decided to drive around the park—the longer, but hassle-free way. Interestingly enough, there were fugitives on the loose from Arizona, and they were caught right where we would have been coming out of Yellowstone that very same day. I guess my angels were protecting us again!

CHAPTER 8

───∿∿⌒⊙⌒∿∿───

Why Oh Why Oh Mee

On my first trip to Wyoming (in 2009)—or should I say, "Why Oh Why Oh Mee" . . .

I was beginning to understand that Bob loves to drive, and sometimes he likes to drive rather long distances. We drove from Scottsdale, Arizona, to Wyoming, and it was minus twenty degrees in Wyoming when we got there, which is way too cold for me. We drove at very high elevations over eight thousand feet. Even though the scenery was beautiful, I was afraid we would go over the edge, for there were no guard rails. In addition, we were misguided by our GPS, which gave us the most direct route and the most challenging, for it was through two mountains, in the middle of a winter snowstorm.

Bob had decided to let Chris, our son, drive. Of all times to eat chips and dip, Chris thought this was it. Chris had a can of nacho cheese dip on the center console of the truck and a bag of chips between his legs. Now, I was very nervous and thought he should have both hands on the wheel instead of dipping chips in cheese dip and eating. All I could think about was that if we went off the road, it would be days before anyone would find us, because we were driving a white truck in a white snowstorm and everything was white.

Bob tried to distract me and told me to watch a movie with him. Knowing that we were driving on black ice (the kind you can't see, for it matches the pavement) on stretches of mountainside where there were no signs of life of any kind and anyone with any sense would not be out on a night like this—I had to ask myself, What the _____ are we doing here?

Despite the nacho eating episode and the black ice, I have to say that Chris is a good driver, for he got us safely to our hotel in Moab, Utah, even if I was an emotional mess. I was happy again to live to tell the story, for it was a long and rough ride to safety after being in such a remote part of the world.

We visited some friends near Jackson Hole and were supposed to go snowmobiling, but with the extreme cold weather and the threat of avalanches, I voted we move on to a warmer location and opted out. I thought Jackson Hole was God's country. While we were in Jackson Hole, I saw elk and moose for the first time.

On our way back to Arizona, we drove through Utah and had a fabulous dinner at a quaint European restaurant called La Caille at Quail Run. Bob was trying to score points with me after that scary drive (and he earned a few that night).

The next day we drove through Arches National Park and took some really great pictures. It was cold, and not many people visit when it is cold. I was impressed with all the magnificent rock formations.

The next day we worked our way over to the Grand Canyon and took a helicopter ride over the canyon, which gave it a whole new dimension.

I think everyone should experience this at least once. On our way back to Scottsdale, we stayed at a haunted hotel (like I hadn't had enough excitement) in a small Arizona town called Jerome. I slept with one eye open, but was happy to report no drama that night.

The next day we would be back in Scottsdale, and I would be warm!

CHAPTER 9

‒‒‒‒‒‒‒‒‒‒‒‒‒‒‒‒‒‒

Montana Rose and Other Gaited Mules

In the fall of 1991, Bob and his good friend Mose Oppenheimer (little Mose grandfather) made a short trip to check out a spotted saddle horse stallion in the hill country near Smokey Valley Farm in Rowan County, Kentucky. As Bob and Mose examined the stallion outside a rustic barn, a twelve-year-old boy, barefoot and dressed in bibbed overalls, rode out of the barn on a tall and leggy two-year-old sorrel mare mule, who was also barefooted. The young mule exited the barn with a running walk and then stepped up into a fast and stylish racking gait. Bob and Mose were both astonished, as they were well aware that mules that were both smooth-gaited and fast were very rare and special. The focus of the horse-trading trip immediately changed to acquiring the young and talented walking mule. After considerable discussion and negotiation, this task was accomplished, and the mule was soon loaded into the horse trailer to begin her new life at Smokey Valley Farm.

Rambling Rose amazed all who rode and watched her with her smooth and perfect gaits and her stunning speed in gait. After three years, Bob decided to sell her, and she was quickly sold at a good price. She went on to win multiple walking mule world championships and became a legend among those who admire great walking mules. After retirement Bob continued his interest in gaited mules, but nearly twenty years passed before another young mule was found of sufficient quality.

In the summer of 2010, Bob was riding his horse Mystic on a friend's ranch in Montana. It was there he spotted a very precocious five-month-old gray mule foal. Her conformation, gaits, and movements were at such a high level that he was immediately convinced he had stumbled upon a fitting successor to Rambling Rose.

Bob spent the next three days negotiating with the rancher to acquire the young mule, which had been hidden out of view on the ranch to minimize the temptation to sell her. The next problem was that the young mule was too young to transport from Montana to Kentucky, as she had not yet been weaned. Bob continued to negotiate a fee for board until he could pick her up the next summer.

When we went back to pick her up the next year, she needed to get some shoes put on. She'd had minimal exposure to humans, however, so when the farrier put shoes on her, she gave him a good kick in the ear. This farrier had a bumper sticker on his car stating that he was the blacksmith from hell. At least he had a personality, for she split his ear open, and he had to go to the emergency room to get stitches. He later put a picture of his ear on Facebook and labeled it "mule tracks."

After careful consideration, we decided to name our new acquisition Montana Rose. I call her Rosie for short. She is now happily in residence at Smokey Valley Farm and was started under saddle in the summer of 2012, and we are very excited about her prospects.

In the past year we have also acquired a matched pair of spotted gaited mules: Jewel, who was five, and Jasper, who was three years old. We trained this pair to ride, drive, and pack.

These mules already have expanded our backcountry range and safety and have added wonderful experiences to our lives.

Have You Heard the Story about a Three-Bell Mule?

In the past, mules were used in the army for important tasks. Since mules could not talk, the officers trimmed their tails in the shape of a bell to inform other officers about the mule's capabilities. One bell meant the mule could be ridden; a second bell meant he could pack; and the third bell meant the mule was capable of being ridden or could be used for packing as well as pulling a wagon.

Olive Hill, Kentucky

I knew absolutely nothing about a mule when we acquired Rosie from Montana. At first it was all about getting acquainted, for she had not been handled much and was used to being in the same corral with her other mule friends about the same age.

The first thing we had to do was separate her from her corral buddies so we could bond with her and get her respect. She cried a lot at first, for she didn't like being alone and missed her companions. I visited her on a daily basis and talked with her, petted her, and brushed her mane. She started to follow me around like a puppy dog. I trimmed her mane and tail and was surprised she let me do it, especially since she had not had much human contact. I quickly fell in love with my new mule friend named Rosie and her magnificent long ears. Rosie taught me a lot about mules in the months to follow. I learned she was very playful, so I got her a ball with a handle on it and tied it to a tree branch. It was fun to watch her spend hours on her hind legs hitting this ball with her front legs and head. Sometimes Rosie would do a spin and hit the ball with a jump and a kick of her hind legs. She is very affectionate and smart and really likes people. She especially likes people who brush, scratch, and feed her.

A mule is the progeny of a male donkey (a jack) and a female horse (a mare). In contrast, the union of a male horse (a stallion) and a female donkey (a jenny) produces a hinny. Hinnies are slightly more horse-like in appearance than mules. Since both mules and hinnies are hybrids, they are sterile. Mules have small but very hard and durable hooves. They are more sure-footed than horses, making them safer in steep and rugged terrain. Mules are tough and can go longer and farther without food and water than horses.

The first time one of our trainers rode Rosie, she really liked it and seemed to catch on quickly to what was expected of her.

Horses versus Mules

Mules are much less likely than horses to injure themselves, have colic, or contract laminitis. They have a hefty sense of self-preservation and rarely go over backward with a rider, run through fences, or injure one another by kicking. If a mule gets a leg caught in a barbed-wire fence, she will either figure out how to free herself without injury or will wait stoically and patiently for help. In the same situation, horses will usually struggle to free their leg and injure themselves severely in the process.

A mule rarely overeats to the point of detriment or drinks too much when overheated. Most mules cannot be "ridden to death," as horses can. If a mule is ridden to the point that she feels her health is in danger, she will stop, perhaps lie down, and refuse to go on until sufficiently rested. If a pack mule is loaded with more weight than she can safely carry, she may lie down or refuse to move.

I know you've heard the expression "stubborn as a mule." Well, I learned the reality of that through Jewel when Bob and I tried to load her into the horse trailer one day. She just did not feel like going in. We learned in training mules that you have to let mules think that what you want them to do is their idea and not yours. A horse can usually be intimidated and forced to do things that he perceives to be either senseless or potentially harmful to himself. Mules think for themselves, and, therefore, you cannot treat them like you do a horse. Mules notice everything on the trail, but once they're trained, very little bothers them. From the donkey, mules gain the wisdom required to evaluate strange situations without a great deal of fear and agitation. Mules very rarely run through fences or cliffs, but rather choose their retreat with concern for their safety. They are much less flight oriented than horses are. Surprisingly, mules have a smooth gait. On one ride I clocked Jewel at fifteen miles per hour. Mules live seven to nine years longer than horses.

Mules have a good memory and do not forget anything. If mistreated, mules will wait until the opportunity arises for them to get even.

I learned that an ordinary saddle will not fit a mule properly. A mule saddle needs either a crupper or a britchin to keep the saddle from slipping forward. The backs of mules are generally flatter than the backs of horses.

When Bob first got Jewel, he put his horse saddle on her and took her for a spin around the riding ring, only to have a wardrobe malfunction. The saddle slipped forward, the breast strap broke, the saddle slide sideways, and the horn of the saddle caught the front of Bob's shirt and tore it open and off his back like out of a Chippendale routine. Everyone watched in amazement as Bob fell in slow motion to the ground. Luckily he had no major injuries other than a mutilated shirt.

Mules will test your horsemanship. You must be patient, kind, gentle, consistent, and very persuasive to train mules and get along well with them.

Interestingly enough, a well-trained mule can be laid up for many weeks or even months and when you go back to ride that mule, it will usually act as if you had ridden it the day before, unlike a horse. I am quickly becoming a mule fan, because I have learned they are less temperamental than horses . . . not to mention that the older you get, the harder it is when you hit the ground.

Mules are the equine version of a sport-utility vehicle. Their sure-footedness and how they move with ease and comfort over and through rugged terrain are amazing to watch. These features are why mules are well suited for traveling the trails of the Grand Canyon. And of course, they can see the placement of their hind feet (horses cannot), a trait that gives them added insurance in taking the right step on steep canyon trails.

Summary

I had a fear of mules, for I knew nothing about them, except they can move their legs in all directions so they have more options to kick you if they want and usually don't miss!

Interestingly enough, the mule that we acquired from Montana, Rosie, is now one of my best friends on the farm.

CHAPTER 10

Time to Cowboy Up!

Personal Journal, August 7, 2010

Lewis and Clark Reenactment (our second time here)

Bob and Chris decided to set out and find the trail that we tried to find the other day when we made a wrong turn. I stayed behind to do chores and get ready for our departure tomorrow to Big Sky. Emily and I would venture off later to see the town shops and a pioneer pottery place.

The boys took off to explore the upper reaches of the Stillwater River Canyon in Montana. The canyon is accessed by taking Nye Road to the end at the Stillwater Trailhead. Bob said that immediately at the beginning of the ride they experienced a mile of formidable rapids and white water below them as they rode on a six-foot-wide passage, and it was quite the Saturday morning wake-up call, for the water was only thirty-eight degrees and the rocks they were riding on were slick.

The horses were still fresh and spirited from a day of rest. Chris and Bob both admitted later that they kept the reins shorter on one side to stay closer to the rock wall than the river below. Bob said it was definitely worth the risk, for the views of the water rushing over the massive-sized boulders were simply fantastic.

On the first three miles of the ride, they met fishermen, runners, hikers, and pets. Apparently folks from Montana don't take the bear signs too seriously! As they continued up the canyon, they were awed by spectacular views of mountain peaks and river vistas. As the vibrant sun glistened on the canyon walls, the tumultuous river flowed below. There were endless possible pictures to be taken.

As they continued up the canyon, each scene rivaled the last. As they went even farther up the trail, they no longer saw others. The main attraction for hikers is a wide spot in the river called Stillwater Lake. After two and a half hours of riding and continuous beautiful scenes, they spotted a small branch trail to the left and then turned around to head back to the ranch.

Now that Bob had discovered Stillwater Canyon and thought it was so magnificent, he wanted to share it with me. Due to prior experiences with my lovely husband, I decided to go with him the day before our ride to check out the trail. At the entrance of the trail, I saw an extremely narrow, rocky, wet path above freezing raging waters. Now, I am an experienced rider. However, this was very intimidating, to say the least. If your horse slipped and you fell in the water, you would die instantly, and they would never find your body.

After I took a big gulp, I looked at Bob and said, "Is there another way in?" After talking with the rangers, we discovered a less intimidating way to get to Stillwater Canyon, and from what we could see, it didn't look too bad.

The next day we had our picnic lunch packed and were ready for our adventure. We started on what was a pleasant ride through the woods, which was a great alternative to the other entrance. But then the trail started getting very unstable and steep, which we had no way of knowing the day before. It seemed like we were heading up on a ninety-degree incline when all of a sudden the rocks were crumbling right out from under our horses' feet. We quickly jumped off our horses and decided the best way to get through this was to walk them up this incline. Bob took my horse first. I saw him fall down, and then the horse dropped to its knees, but they both got back up. I quickly followed behind, and it was all I could do to walk on this rough surface of boulders and small rocks without falling over. The challenge of climbing and getting short of breath with physical exercise seems twice as hard in high altitude. We finally made it to the top of the mountain and continued down into the canyon on a windy, rocky trail.

We traveled through fields of flowers, and it was all very beautiful, but I felt like I was on sensory overload, for there was so much to think about—not to mention the threat of wildlife approaching at any given moment. Above, the snow-capped mountains surrounded us, and in the canyon were vividly colored flowers. There was so much beauty to take in all at once while watching my horse's footing to stay on this narrow trail at such a high altitude. Whew! I can see why Bob wanted me to see this special place.

By now my back was starting to give out from all the pounding and stress of getting into the canyon. We found the perfect spot to sit and be with nature and have lunch. I was struggling to eat my lunch, however, for I was already wondering how I would make the ride back.

As we were finishing lunch, it seemed like clumps of cold moisture were falling on us. We realized then that we had forgotten to bring our rain gear, so we had to be creative. We had some bright orange emergency sleeping bags, so we cut those in half and made slits for our head and arms. Just as we put them on, the chunky stuff falling from the sky turned to hail, and it hurt as it hit our bodies. We had nowhere to seek shelter, so we kept riding in hopes it would stop soon.

After about forty-five minutes, it stopped and the sun came out again, which helped warm us up. I hung in as best I could and was very much looking forward to getting off my horse and taking a warm shower. Bob's horse Mystic threw a shoe. Luckily we had an easy boot with us, so we found a spot to stop and put it on.

On the way back, we had to go up one big mountain with more loose rocks than the first one. When I saw Bob get off his horse to walk it up the hill and they both fell to their knees, I turned to Bob and said, "I am not going that way." Bob came to get my horse and took it up the loose, rocky terrain. Then he came back for me and walked me out the other way. The other riders we were with watched our horses until Bob returned. Bob gave me a personal escort over the slick wet rocks above the raging cold waters, which was the only other way out. I stayed as close as I could to the rock wall and prayed a lot for our safety. Once we made it to the entrance, I went to our horse trailer and waited for Bob to come back with our horses and the other riders. What an adventure. Next stop, a chiropractor!

White-Water Rafting on the Snake River

We stayed at the Spotted Horse Ranch in Jackson Hole, Wyoming, and one of our adventures was a white-water rafting trip. We had a choice of a scenic ride or an adventure ride. Well, which one do you think Bob picked? That's right, the adventure ride. He said the scenic ride would be too boring. I nervously agreed to do the adventure white-water rafting trip, not knowing exactly what I was getting myself into. We were given wet suits, for the water was extremely cold and would be dangerous if we fell in. We were then loaded on a bus and driven to the Snake River. All I could wonder was what would happen next.

When the bus got us to our destination, we were then taken close to our loading area to get on the raft. Each of us was given a life jacket and a paddle. Next, we had to climb into the raft and get in position. This required an awkward turn with your butt hanging off the side of the raft. For me, it was a difficult and uncomfortable position, for my back was still stiff from the Stillwater Canyon ride. As the guide explained that we had to put one foot in a loop on the floor to anchor us in the raft, I wondered how I would last in this awkward and painful position for the next hour.

I attempted paddling, but the guide singled me and a few others out, saying that if we did not paddle harder, we would flip over. On that note, I had a meltdown and turned in my paddle. I knew that with my back hurting as badly as it did, I was not able to paddle harder at this time. Luckily, a rambunctious sixteen-year-old was elated to take my position on the raft. We switched seats, and soon I was in the center of the raft next to a cute six-year-old and feeling a little more comfortable.

Just as I was thinking this could be fun, the guide started acting like we were in boot camp. He yelled at the people in the front of the raft. He said they were not paddling hard enough and that they shouldn't stop every time they got splashed (with the ice-cold water). Now it started to get intense, for the guide warned us that due to high amounts of snowfall last winter, this river was running extremely high. He said that several rafts had turned over in the last two weeks. He then continued to tell us that someone died just last week when he fell out of the boat.

The guide was getting us ready for a really big wave that was coming our way. Then, as I looked at the raft in front of us, someone fell out. Just as we hit the really big wave, Bob lost his footing and fell off the side and inside the raft. Bob had a heck of a time getting back up on the side of the raft, for we were getting pounded by water on all sides, and it was a cold and very rough ride. By this time, I was taking some serious deep breaths, for the guide continued to tell us a hundred ways we were going to die today. As we hit the next big wave, the little boy next to me looked at me and said, "Are we going to die?" I had to take a deep breath before I could answer him. After I sighed, I held him and said, "I sure hope not!" Then our whole raft was engulfed by an enormous wake, and everyone was soaked with the icy water, even with wet suits on.

Our drill sergeant guide continued to terrorize us with stories about people falling off and trying to stand up, only to get their feet stuck under rocks on the bottom of the river. This was one time I thought I might not live until the end of one of our adventures. This was, after all, my first rafting experience and probably would be my last. Talk about being stretched out of one's comfort zone!

When we finally made it to our stopping point, I hopped out of that raft as fast as I could. It had emotionally drained me, and it took me a day or so to recover from the so-called adventure—which I paid for?

Survival Is Surely a Motivator

This was my last day in Jackson Hole before I flew back to Kentucky, so Bob and I decided to go for one last trail ride. We brought along a friend who had been a wrangler at one time and was familiar with the backcountry. Bob was excited about using his new compact fly-fishing reel, and he would just piece it together once we found a good fishing spot off the trail. We packed our picnic lunch and hit the backcountry. We climbed some rugged terrain to get to a mountaintop that was covered with bright yellow flowers. We decided this was a good scenic lunch spot, and so we stopped for a lunch break.

After lunch we headed down the mountain to a stream to try our hand at fishing with Bob's new pole. It was great in that the minute he cast his line he caught a beautiful trout; it was a big one, but we released him. After a few more nibbles it seemed like the fish had disappeared, so I suggested we head back, because it looked like the afternoon showers were headed our way.

We had more rugged terrain to go through to get back to the dude ranch, and I wondered how novice riders got through this challenging trail. Several times we were on very narrow paths with over a hundred-foot drop below us. In case you didn't know, horses cannot see the placement of their back feet like a mule can, which can be crucial at a time like this. At one point in the trail the horse in front of me lost his footing on his back legs, and I got nervous, for I thought he was going to go off the cliff. After watching him nervously shuffle to get his back legs on the trail again, I took a deep breath of relief. Shortly after that, my horse started losing her footing as well, and I gasped as I tried to redirect her to get all four feet on the path.

Within seconds after I got all four of my horse's feet back on the path, I heard two loud bangs in back of me. As I turned around, I saw Bob's horse go over the cliff edge, but I did not see Bob! At that moment I was in sheer terror, wondering where he was. I didn't know if he was under the horse or somewhere hanging off the side below me. We were on a very narrow path, so there was nowhere to turn around to even get off my horse, so I continued forward on the path to look for a wide spot. Since there wasn't a wide spot I swung my leg over the back of my horse and stood on one stirrup to get a better view and look for Bob. That's when I saw him lying facedown on the narrow trail. Somehow he'd jumped off just as the horse went over the cliff. I yelled out to him, "Are you okay?" We couldn't believe the close call he'd just had. He said he was fine as he dusted himself off and got up slowly, with nothing broken and only a few scrapes on his arm.

Then I noticed Bob's horse. By some miracle its back end had landed on an aspen tree, and it was struggling to get its footing to climb back to us. Believe it or not, when I called her name, that horse was able to get its footing and climb back to us on the trail. She came to me, and I quickly grabbed her reins and pulled her on the trail in front of me, since it was too narrow for two horses side by side. I yelled out with relief to Bob, "I got her," and he walked over to get his horse. By the grace of God and all the angels above, both Bob and the horse came out of this with minor scratches. Talk about living on the edge!

It was a quiet ride the rest of the way to the ranch, and we were just so grateful for a happy ending. Just think, we were located where there is no cell service, so I would not have been able to call for help. Instead, I would have sent the wrangler for help and stayed behind in hopes no wildlife would come by and make me its prey!

CHAPTER 11

The Highway to Heaven

Personal Journal, August 3, 2010

We drove through a town called Red Lodge on our way to Absarokee, Montana. Red Lodge had several great restaurants and western wear shops. We found a breakfast place we really liked called Prindis Place. After Red Lodge we discovered the highway to heaven, also known as Beartooth

Highway. This road goes south from Red Lodge to the northern entrance of Yellowstone National Park at the Wyoming/Montana border. The sides of the rock on some of the curves on this windy drive are coated with cement to keep the rock from sliding onto the road. In other areas we saw thick, heavy metal netting to hold sliding rocks.

I'm getting queasy again as we gain altitude . . . probably not a good idea to eat before doing this drive. I would, however, recommend having a camera on hand, for it is a great photo opportunity. Remember to take deep breaths as well. You will see what it is like to be on top of the world! I'd say this brings a whole new meaning to the expression "living high." It was fifty-nine degrees on top, and there was a big plateau—this road is a great ride for a motorcycle. We saw vibrant purple and yellow wildflowers against the dark brown mountain color.

Did I tell you what Montana means? It is Spanish for mountains. When we were getting close to the top of the mountain, we saw sticks added to posts to increase their height. We found out these were to measure the height of the snow, which could be as high as ten feet. They also have warning gates (sort of look like a toll gate) that close when the snow gets too deep. We entered Wyoming—and by the way, who forgot to tell Wyoming about guardrails on the roads? These roads are truly steep and windy, definitely not for drinking and driving after dark. This drive blows the one at the Grand Canyon away. The views are incredible! Just when you think you are at the top, you go higher still. It is amazing to see snow in August, and we watched kids playing in the distance running barefoot, playing on the rocks, and then posing for a picture.

We just passed a sign that says we are at eleven thousand feet elevation. We saw road crews clearing rock slides, and I had to laugh when I saw a worker holding a sign that said "Slow." That would not be taken lightly here. I thought it was interesting to see how the wildflowers pop up in the dirt and rocks against the mountainsides. The road continues like the shape of a snake through the mountaintops. I have a picture of this on our GPS, which is rather unusual. We saw glacial lakes on top of the mountains. This drive took us about an hour, and it was a powerful hour. The air is so crisp and fresh—no pollution here. We are now in grizzly bear country.

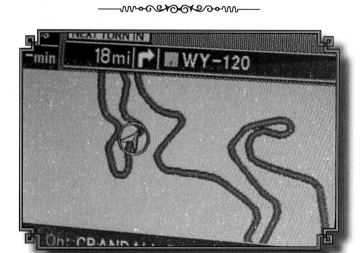

Next we drove on the Chief Joseph Scenic Highway to Cody, Wyoming, which is another scenic drive with a story behind it. As we are driving, we pass a herd of longhorn cattle. It is motorcycle mania here. We are seeing so many motorcycles heading to Sturgis, South Dakota, for their annual gathering, where thousands of motorcycle enthusiasts will party hearty for a week.

As we continue our drive along this famous highway, we see a beautiful stream running along the roadside among the various rocks. Chief Joseph was a legendary fearless leader of over a couple thousand Indians called the Nez Perce tribe, who took this path on their Appaloosa horses in attempts to outrun the army. The army was forcing the Indians to say on reservations, where they were disrespected and given poor food. Indians that refused to stay on the reservations were considered rebels. The Nez Perce Indians outfought the US Calvary in 1877. They were fighting for freedom, after Custer's last stand.

Chief Joseph led his people from Idaho and the Salmon River country through Wyoming and Montana just short of the Canadian border. Although they made it to Canada, they were forced to live on a reservation, and it was ordered that all their Appaloosa horses be killed because the army did not want to chase those fast horses again. Chief Joseph was a peaceful man. But since he was forced to live on a reservation, he died of a broken heart.

High-Altitude Sickness

I couldn't understand why I kept feeling so queasy, had headaches, and lost my appetite. My girlfriend in Big Sky said she usually had strange dreams every time she visited Montana. I later found out the most common manifestations of altitude sickness are headache, nausea, loss of appetite, insomnia, wakeful sleep and strange dreams, lethargy, and sometimes a warm or flushed feeling in the face. It usually lasts one or two days. Resting, especially during the first few days, eating lightly, drinking more liquids, and limiting alcohol intake will help significantly.

Diamox is a prescription medication that can be prescribed by your doctor. The usual dosage is 250 milligrams twice daily, two days before arrival and the first two days while you're there. I will have to remember this for our next trip here.

Swelling

Otherwise symptomless swelling of the face, hands, and feet, with a weight gain of four to twelve pounds, sometimes occurs at high altitude, most often in women. I experienced these symptoms as well. The swelling may persist for several days after one returns to lower altitude before it resolves spontaneously. The cause is unknown, but the condition will respond to a low-salt diet and diuretics.

Altitude Effects on Medical Problems

People with chronic lung or heart disease may be adversely affected by high elevation. The presence of less oxygen changes body functions, making it harder to breathe and forcing the heart to work harder. Your pulse will be faster at higher altitudes than it would be in lower elevations, so you must adjust your pace to avoid overexertion. I found things like just walking at this high elevation were an effort, so I had to reduce my activity level.

Dehydration

Dehydration is very common due to the marked dryness of the high mountain air combined with the increased breathing rate from less oxygen. This results in increased body loss of moisture, which can be much greater with alcohol consumption. A healthy adult should drink at least six to eight glasses of water daily, especially out west.

CHAPTER 12

———⌇⌇⌇∘◦⟲⟩∘◦⟨⟲∘◦⌇⌇⌇———

Don't Dream About the Wild West—Live It!

Cody, Wyoming

The town of Cody was like out of an old western movie. We stayed at the Chamberlin Inn, a boutique-type place. Our next stop was to meet up with Keith Seidel at his saddle shop in town. He gave my saddle a complete tune-up, and I didn't even know there was such a thing. While my saddle was being worked on, Bob and I decided to visit the Buffalo Bill Historical Center, which was great!

It is the finest museum in North America. It comprises five museums, all with western themes. These museums include Western Art, with pieces by well-known artists such as Russell and Remington. Another museum focuses on the Plains Indians. Of course, there's also a Buffalo Bill museum, with items related to the life of Buffalo Bill Cody. I had my picture taken with a Buffalo Bill impersonator.

The Greater Yellowstone Natural History museum reproduces high-altitude subalpine terrain and wildlife, including an amazing preserved wolverine and grizzly bear. The Draper Museum of Natural History at the Buffalo Bill Historical Center also has the finest personal firearms collection in the world in yet another wing.

Triple Creek Ranch

We retraced our steps to Bozeman, Montana, and then we went southwest to Darby. Darby is a very small town outside of Triple Creek Ranch (TCR). TCR is a high-end dude ranch that specializes in cattle drives and horseback riding. Everyone was amazed that we brought our own horses. The ranch had only quarter horses. In Kentucky, we say friends don't let friends ride trotting horses. I had a quarter horse before I met Bob, but after injuring my back in a car accident, I thought it would never be possible for me to ride again—that is, until I tried a Tennessee walker and felt the difference and the smoothness in the ride.

The food at the TCR was one of the highlights, and we looked forward to enjoying the creativeness of the chef and the presentation of the meals.

Boulder Creek Ride

A cowboy must have named this trail, for it had a creek running along most of the path amid many boulders. In the middle of the trail was a cascading waterfall that was tranquil and refreshing. It was another emotional ride for me, for the path was narrow, approximately fifteen to eighteen inches wide. On one side was the drop-off, and on the other were boulders piled up as high as one could see along the mountainside. There was not a cloud in the sky, and we had a strong breeze today. When the wind would blow, I could get a whiff of the evergreen trees.

Step by step, Hombre strategically placed his hooves, carefully stepping through these boulders. Occasionally we would slide, but he always caught his balance. We had aluminum shoes on our horses so we would have a better grip on this rocky terrain. I even traded in my cowgirl hat for a top-of-the-line riding helmet by Troxel. We bought easy boots as a backup in case any of the horses lost a shoe.

Due to the dryness of the Montana air, the nails were starting to loosen in Hombre's shoes. I applied hoof conditioner every day, for his hooves were cracking and crumbling due to the ruggedness of the terrain. Bob checked Hombre's shoes before our ride that day, and they seemed fine. Bob and I made it to the top of Boulder Creek, where we had a picnic lunch. Chipmunks joined us as our lunch buddies. These chipmunks were rather brave, even attempting to open our ziplock bags we'd placed on the rocks. They tried to get inside them to eat our sandwiches.

We sat on the rocks and looked at the creek that had followed us all the way up the mountain, as well as the beauty of the mountains in the distance. During lunch I had to regroup and think about doing this daring ride again, only going down this time.

Somehow, going down seemed to take much longer than going up. By the time we got back down the trail, I had to use the restroom. I hooked Hombre to our horse trailer and ran to an outside bathroom. On the outside of the door was a big sign that read, "Warning: Bears have been sighted in this area. Proceed with caution." Before our ride we were also told about the abundance of wolves and moose that were around as well. I took care of business rather quickly. Luckily for us, we did not have any wildlife encounters on this ride.

Oh, So That's How You Do It?

I had never been fly-fishing before, so I was excited to learn. Bob and I took a lesson to learn how to fly-fish before we went out with the guide we hired. We were on the West Fork of the Bitterroot River. This guide took us in his boat with his dog, who also liked to fish. Bob had fly-fished before, so he was really eager to skip the lesson and get started. As the guide continued to do his lesson, Bob cast his line and hooked a nineteen-inch hybrid rainbow trout that weighed about four pounds. The guide decided it was time to end the lesson and start fishing, for, according to him, this was the biggest catch of the week. It was a catch and release, so we took a picture and documented our catch before we released it.

I forgot to mention the guide's black Lab was in the front of the boat with me, and he was starting to get in my way. I like dogs, but this one was stealing the moment and peacefulness from our adventure, not to mention fish. I had hooked a big one and was stripping my line to bring the fish to the boat. As I was about to get the fish in the net, the Lab jumped out of the boat and knocked the guide over. The net in his hands tipped, and there went my fish.

At one point Bob had me hooked—literally. His hook grabbed my hand, and I felt the tension in my hand and told him not to pull anymore. I pulled the hook out of my hand, and we continued fishing. I was amazed that we couldn't see the fish, as clear as the water was. We were able to catch three fish that day. Two were sixteen to eighteen inches long, and one was eighteen to nineteen inches. We had a great day with beautiful weather as we learned how to fly-fish, and we gained knowledge we can put to use in the future.

We went a full week at Triple Creek without cell service. At first it was frustrating, but then it became liberating. We stayed in a designer log cabin, if there is such a thing, and it met both our needs. On the inside it was luxurious, and on the outside it looked rugged. I liked the Jacuzzi on the porch in the back of our cabin and put it to good use.

We made some new friends, including a young couple from Germany who just got married in Vegas before they arrived here for their honeymoon. We spent time together getting to know each other, including having meals together.

We learned TCR is really for people who don't have access to horses or knowledge and skills for these ventures. We enjoyed seeing the private western collection of Craig and Barbara Barrett, the owners of TCR, as well as their nearby 27,000-acre CB Ranch. We took a private ride with Craig and Barbara and helped get the kinks out of her horse, which was misbehaving. Along the ride, I saw part of the lower leg of an elk on our trail, which was evidence of a previous wolf attack. We also learned that Craig Barrett was a former CEO and chairman of Intel.

We enjoyed breathtaking mountain vistas and an abundance of wildlife, such as herds of elk and deer. We never saw a mountain lion, but we did see a dead wolf. The weather was mostly in the eighties, and we had daylight until almost 9 p.m. in the evening. We saw many wild and rather large turkeys roaming the property at TCR.

Personal Journal, August 26, 2010
(This is our second trip)

We are leaving the Triple Creek Ranch and are now heading through Idaho on the way to Jackson Hole, Wyoming. Just south of Jackson Hole, we found a great place for our horses. I was seriously ready for a day of retail therapy, so instead of riding we decided to go into town.

It appeared that most of the shops had overpriced tourist stuff. We stopped and had a cold beer at a famous cowboy bar, which had actual saddles at the bar to sit on instead of bar stools. Jackson Hole is a relatively large valley, but roads are few, and getting around is fairly easy. Through known to have an arid climate, Jackson Hole is subject to extreme and fluctuating weather patterns in both summer and winter.

We were staying at the Four Seasons Hotel. The funniest part was realizing that our dually was covered with mud and dirt from the drive, but we drove up as if we had a beautiful Bentley. When they opened our doors to help us unload, loose items fell everywhere from out of our truck. As embarrassing as that was, I did not care, for I was back in civilization by the Tetons and had a room with a great view. We had a romantic dinner the next night at a restaurant at the top of the mountain at Teton Village, and we had to take a sky lift to get there.

Grand Teton National Park

This park was established in 1929 to protect peaks and lakes in the Teton Range, and additional open space was secured along the valley floor in 1950. The mountains were named "les trois Tetons" (the three breasts) by the French.

By the early nineteenth century, thanks to fur trappers, the Tetons became the focal point—at heights up to 13,772 feet—of an incredible recreation and conservation area. The Teton mountain range is young by geologic standards—only approximately nine million years of age—and runs forty miles long by 12 miles wide, flanked by the Snake River. Don't miss the Snake River overlook, just one of the numerous turnouts along the northeast route between Moran Junction and Moose Junction. Many consider this the best spot to see a panoramic view of the Tetons.

We had seen horse-drawn sleigh rides through the National Elk Refuge the last time we were there. Archeological evidence reveals that bands of paleo-Indians made summer camps near the Tetons soon after the last major ice age ended, about ten thousand years ago. It appears that they used the valley primarily to harvest its meadows of wild plants for their edible roots and seeds. The valley's animal populations were hunted for their meat and skins. Historian still ponder why these early bands of people left the area between AD 1000 and 1600, only to be replaced by today's more commonly known tribes of Shoshone, Crow, Gros Ventre, and Blackfoot.

Each year from about 1820 to 1840, trappers, hunters, and traders from throughout the Rocky Mountains gathered at predetermined valleys to exchange the season's furs for equipment, tobacco, whiskey, and news of the outside world. These events were known as rendezvous, from the French word for "appointment" or "meeting place."

While Jackson Hole never held one of these big two-week gatherings, mountain men would use the distinctive Teton range as a landmark meeting place before heading to the more hospitable Pierre's Hole or Green River rendezvous sites. After Lewis and Clark's Corps of Discovery Expedition passed near Jackson Hole and headed eastward in late 1806, member John Colter stayed in the West to join some hunters in probing the upper Yellowstone River for beaver. Their efforts were apparently less than rewarding, and Colter parted amicably with the trappers the following spring to return alone to civilization.

Teton Village Trails

Located at the gateway to Grand Teton National Park, Teton Village and the Jackson Hole Mountain Resort Aerial Tram provide access to amazing hiking trails, ranging from moderately easy to strenuous. Ride the tram 4,139 vertical feet to the top of Rendezvous Mountain while experiencing 360-degree aerial views of the surrounding Tetons and Snake River Valley.

Yellowstone National Park

This park is home to more than two hundred species of animals. The wildlife you see in the park depends on when you visit and what part of the park you are in, as well as what time of day and the weather.

The landscape has been and is being created by many geological forces. Here, some of the earth's most active volcanic hydrothermal (water and heat) and earthquake systems make this national park a priceless treasure. Yellowstone was established as the world's first national park primarily because of its unparalleled collection of geysers, hot springs, mud pots, and steam vents.

Mud pots are acidic features with a limited water supply. Their consistency and activity vary with the seasons and precipitation. Old Faithful is the most geologically active geyser.

The Continental Divide is a high point that runs through Yellowstone. Ironically, if a drop of water could split in half here, half of it could go to the Pacific Ocean and half to the Gulf of Mexico.

We were heading to Colorado now, and by now Hombre's shoes had worn thin and his hooves were crumbling more from the dryness. We were heading to our last stop of this journey and would have to find a farrier to get some new shoes for Hombre. It was pouring rain when we arrived at the dude ranch where we were staying near Steamboat Springs in Colorado.

We got our horses unloaded and settled in, and then we scrambled to get our collection of luggage inside, despite the heavy rainfall. I didn't have a good feeling about this dude ranch, for it was run-down and the woman who ran the place was rude. When they showed us the room, my heart sank with disappointment, and all I could think about was being at home in my comfortable bed.

We quickly learned that many families were visiting this ranch the week we stayed. It seemed like a gazillion kids were on the loose, and most of the functions and meals were also geared toward kids. We kept busy with our horses and entertained ourselves. We took a trail ride on the side of a mountain and through what seemed like a forest of aspen trees. It was so magical to ride our Tennessee Walkers through fields of green. As our horses walked, we felt like we were drifting through these fields. As we rode, we felt like we were in virgin territory, for nothing was disturbed by humans, and there were no signs of litter. We saw an old barn and rode around it and were amazed it was still standing. We then went across an old bridge made from old railroad ties that was equally amazing. We had a picnic lunch by a stream, and everything was serene until one of the horses spooked and tried to break away. We got up quickly from the log we were sitting on and retied our horse so we could return to our bottle of wine and picnic lunch. The rest of the ride was quiet, and we returned on the same mountain path we came from.

The next day we had to get our truck repaired, for we needed a new air filter due to all the dust we had encountered in Wyoming. While the truck was being serviced, we walked around the downtown area in Steamboat and found the people were very friendly. We bought some western wear, and I found a great pair of boots that were cocoa brown with a turquoise pattern on them. We had lunch in a restaurant located right on the river, with the ski slopes in the background. It was a romantic setting with very good food.

We located a farrier while our truck was being serviced for our long journey home to Kentucky, and we headed back to the ranch when the truck was finished. We met the farrier, and he gave Hombre a new set of shoes. We were amazed at the job he did, and he was so fast compared to what we were used to.

The next morning we were headed to the barn when a mule deer came out of nowhere and hopped toward Bob and me as we were walking and holding hands. The mule deer came right at us. Bob skirted to the side rather quickly, and the mule deer kept right on hopping along. I have to say I had never seen a mule deer; it's a good thing he was cute. These mule deer have big ears and dark brown or black tails.

It was interesting to see the many different birds and their vivid colors we noted along the way as we drove. I saw many magpies. They are black and white and seemed to be a fairly good size.

The West has a gift to give you, if you let it happen. It's a place where you can listen for silence and find it. You can live in the moment and truly feel your feet on the ground. It's a kind of magical, spiritual moment . . . a different form of meditation.

During the time I have spent with Bob, I have been challenged to grow. And although some experiences were extremely scary at the time, I am a different person now and approach things much differently than I did before. I am more confident and comfortable in a country environment now, and we have enriched the lives of one another because we share the positives of our different worlds.

We never completely destroy our fears, but with acquired skills and knowledge we can understand situations better.

People have much fear and many misconceptions about bears. We want to replace that with knowledge and respect. Many people don't realize just how wild the backcountry around Yellowstone National Park truly is, yet it's still accessible.

I am still afraid of grizzly bears, but at least I can now ride through where they live and know what to do if we have a bear encounter. They do live in the most beautiful places.

As humans, we are encouraged to get away from our senses. In the wild, our sense of smell sharpens, as well as our eyesight and hearing. We then have a better experience because we are paying more attention. Be prepared, but don't be afraid to wing it—you might be surprised by how good it feels.

It took me two years to appreciate the freedom of not having to be anywhere. After working most of my life, now I choose where I want to be.

Bob on Colorado

Smokey Valley Farm

Smokey Valley Farm is a gathering place for those who pursue excellence in breeding, training, and enjoying gaited saddle horses.

Shadow, Stallion at Smokey Valley Farm

Breeding Program

For more than twenty years, representatives of the finest bloodlines of the Tennessee walking horse have been acquired for the farm's unique breeding program. While a number of world champion Tennessee walking horses have been produced by our breeding stock, the single-minded goal has been to produce extraordinary light-shod traveling horses. The farm's current breeding program started with Prides Persuasion, Blak Power's Jezebelle, and Bomar's Painted Lady in 1987. Later on we added another mare family with the acquisition of Pusher to the Wire. These lines have gone on to produce the heart of our current breeding stock.

Smokey Valley Farmhouse